T0209141

THE MYSTERY OF LIFE

DR. TANYI EYONGETAH

WestBow Press books may be ordered through booksellers or by contacting:

WestBow Press
A Division of Thomas Nelson & Zondervan
1663 Liberty Drive
Bloomington, IN 47403
www.westbowpress.com
1 (866) 928-1240

ISBN: 978-1-9736-9329-1 (sc)
ISBN: 978-1-9736-9328-4 (e)

Print information available on the last page.

WestBow Press rev. date: 06/01/2020

DEDICATION

To my late Grand-father, Samuel Eyongetah, the man who brought Christianity to Tali and many other Upper Banyang villages; and to my mother, Paulina Bessem Tanyi, the woman who delivered me into this present world.

CONTENTS

INTRODUCTION

Many people will ask the question, "what is THE MYSTERY OF LIFE"? It is simply an understanding of the meaning of life that can only be found in Christ. When you turn to God and believe in Him, He will start revealing to you what life is all about. This can only be found in the Bible. The Bible is rich with hidden truths that can be revealed to you as a believer. When you depend, believe, and meditate over the Word of God, it will reveal hidden truths to you.

I decided to write this book in order to share my experiences from the Word of God, in how I have been led in the spirit throughout these years, through a thorough study of the Bible. I have lived a life of turbulence, hatred, hardship, rejection, being poisoned often, yet surviving, slandered by my own family and also by women married in the family, yet my God is still assuring me till today. The only thing that has kept me going in this life has been my dependence on God and His directions. If there was no God, I do not think I would have been alive today. Throughout this pulsating and arduous life, I have been in constant search for the meaning of life. I had asked myself why things happen to me like this. Is there any way out of it?

When I finally was admitted to the University of Port Harcourt in Nigeria, I started developing a philosophy of life, when I read a book written by Betram Russell, entitled *"Why there is no God."*

When I looked back at the pains I was going through, I said, "Truly, if there is a God, I will not go through this." I was carried away by the arguments of Russell, and I was prepared to defend his philosophical point of view to the extent that I did not want to have anything to do with any Christian.

How did things change to the point that I am now the preacher of the gospel? In 1983, I had a dream. In that dream, I died, and after three days, I woke up in that very dream, and started preaching the gospel. When I woke up in the morning, I wondered what this dream could mean. I was frightened because I thought I will die. However, one of my friends spoke to me, and said it is God who is calling me. He prayed for me and gave me a Bible. From that time, I started going to church, and searching the New Testament every day. The teachings of the Lord Jesus Christ were very fascinating to me. When finally, I met students of the Christian Union, they invited me, and from there, I started attending Bible studies. Those studies grounded me in Scriptures until I finally graduated from the university.

After the convocation ceremony, I decided to go home. My father died in January 3, 1987, and I had no reason to stay in Nigeria. I had to go back to Cameroon to take care of my mom. I truly believed that with my university education, I will obtain a good job, and take care of my mother.

Unfortunately, it was the contrary. When I was leaving Nigeria, the Lord gave me two revelations. First, "Go to Cameroon and blow my trumpet, and I will make you part of my people." Second, "You are going to face a lot of difficulties, but look towards me, and I will make you part of my people." I left Nigeria with vistas of knowledge, but it was now for me to apply it, and live by what I have learned from God's Word.

During my arrival in Cameroon, a door was opened to me in prison, where I started preaching the gospel. The mysteries of God were now revealed to my understanding, just as it is written in the Bible:

"But as it is written, eye hath not seen, nor ear heard, neither have entered into the heart of man the things which God hath prepared for them that love him. But God hath revealed them unto us by his Spirit: for the Spirit searcheth all things, yea, the deep things of God" (1 Corinthians 2:9-10 KJV).

There was something I learned about the Bible; you can be very knowledgeable concerning the Word of God, but there are certain mysteries that can only be understood through fasting, prayers, and the purity of your heart. When we receive the Lord Jesus Christ as our personal Savior, God's divine revelation of all people, at all times, will now be revealed to you. It should be noted here that there are two types of revelations; general and special. *General Revelation,* according to Lewis and Demarest, refers to the disclosure of God in nature, through providential history, and in moral law within the heart where people gain an understanding about the God of the universe. *Special Revelation,* on the other hand, is God revealing himself to us through miracles and prophets, which lead us to understand God's way of life.

My attention here is on special revelation, in which Christians can grow deeper in the spirit, through fasting, prayers, meditation, and the Word of God. It is through this process that God starts to use his people to carry out extra-ordinary miracles that cannot be understood by the natural man or nominal Christian.

A study of the New Testament teaches us that the man who received the greatest revelation was Paul. In his Pauline Epistles, First Corinthians is the source of that revelation knowledge. Paul is unchallenged in the revelations he received, not because he was an apostle, but because he went as far as he could go with the Lord to receive everything God had for him. Every child of God who has been chosen must always go as far as he can go in order to receive that deeper revelation which God has for him or her. This book tries to put together how God planned everything for us humans, and how we can tap into that deep revelation, enjoy that life in the Spirit, live a successful life, and learn how to fulfill God's purpose in our lives.

As we will read through this book, let us compare what is written in it, and what is in the Bible. I will want us to identify these truths with our own eyes and in our own Bible. Let us allow the Holy Spirit to lead us to identify these hidden truths.

Paul wrote the first book to the Corinthian church because they were feeding on milk, and not on the meat, which is the Word of God. The apostle Paul describes them as "CARNAL." Let us examine what Paul was saying to the church in 1 Corinthians 3:4-5:

"For while one saith, I am of Paul; and another, I am of Apollos; are ye not carnal? Who then is Paul, and who then is Apollos, but ministers by whom ye believed, even as the Lord gave to every man?"

The apostle Paul is making it succinctly clear that every Christian has a calling! It is through that calling that we have been saved (verse 5). In other words, I came and made you a born again Christian, which planted you into God's Kingdom. In (verse 6), Paul continues to inform them that, "I have planted" (you received salvation through my ministry), "Apollos watered" (he came to impart knowledge), "but God gave the increase." In other words, the Corinthian Christians were to walk according to the biblical principles that they learned from their teachers. Apollos taught about faith and our inheritance in Christ.

Paul was instructing the Corinthian church to focus on the ministry of the Holy Spirit, which will lead to a transformation of their lives and not on man's doctrine which will hold them captive. They are to depend on the leading of the Holy Spirit.

Paul went further to clarify his position in Christ. We are common men like you through whom you have believed the gospel. I cannot do anything above what God has imparted into me. I can only preach salvation and healing onto you, but God is the one who saves and heals you.

It is the same thing that is happening in our churches today. It is very sad how various doctrines have blinded the minds of people, and many have deviated from what the Bible actually teaches. The Baptists have their own doctrine, the Episcopalians and evangelicals have theirs; while the neo-orthodox, Roman Catholics, and other denominations have developed their own type of doctrines as well. People have been blinded by the doctrines of their denominations, rather than reading and understanding what God is really teaching in his Word. The Bible says in Revelation 22:19:

"And if any man shall take away from the words of the book of this prophecy, God shall take away his part out of the book of life, and out of the holy city, and from the things which are written in this book."

The spirit of deceit has permeated the church for centuries and the sad situation is that we are: "Ever learning and never able to come to the knowledge of the truth" (2 Timothy 3:7).

False teachings have now become the norm in our various denominations. The truth has been swept under the carpet, and by so doing, Satan has been winning tremendously. I believe that it is our duty to win back what has been taken away. I know it is not easy to unlearn people from their various denominational teachings, and face the truth from the Bible, and what it really teaches. Many feel that it is a ploy to take them from their church.

It is my hope that this book will lead many people to understand why God created humans, and why it is important to listen to the voice of God, and to be led by His Spirit.

MAN'S CREATION AND THE KINGDOM OF GOD

The first chapter of the Bible teaches us that God meticulously created the world and saw that it was very beautiful. The next question that came forth was, who will take care of what God has created? In Genesis 1:26, God said, "Let Us make man in our image, after our likeness: and let them have dominion over the fish of the sea, and over the fowl of the air, and over the cattle, and over all the earth, and over every living thing that creepeth upon the earth."

Prior to the creation of man, there were angels who had been in existence, even before the world was created. Yet God did not choose them, but felt that man should take charge of His creation. There should be a special reason for this. God does not do things randomly. He has a special purpose for creating man. The reason for doing this was because God wanted somebody to take charge of His creation. Man was on earth to take charge of what He created, and God was in heaven presenting to man everything He created and man was to respect that agreement. For man to take care of what God has created, means that God gave to man enormous power and intellect to take care of the Earth. Man was to rule the Earth according to God's plan. To rule means that there is a territory that God has presented to man to extend his rulership here on Earth. God is in heaven and man is on Earth taking dominion over what has been handed over to him by his Creator.

As we saw in Genesis 1:26, God created the world and mankind to fulfil His eternal purpose here on Earth. The physical Kingdom of God was now handed over to man to take charge and rule in such a way that it reflects God's image here on earth. This type of government meant that God wants to develop a special relationship with man. It should be noted that God is not trying to impose a form of religion. Our Creator is interested in developing a relationship with man, in which man has to look to the invisible God for direction, and man's life has to be dependent solely on God and no one else.

For a man to take care of God's creation, it means that man is called upon to administer over what God has created. As a ruler, man has dominion over what God has allotted to him, and he must rule according to God's will. God has given man special talents and abilities, and there is a written constitution, which is the Word of God, and man is to obey it to the latter, in order to govern the Earth and fulfill God's plan. This was the original intention of creating the Earth. It is a place where God will extend His authority to man from heaven, and man's way of ruling must reflect God's righteousness, character, and wisdom. He was to accomplish God's purpose and plan for the Earth.

If we compare with the governments of the world today, a prime minister or president in any nation, is elected by the people, and given a mandate in any nation to rule for a period before another election is held with other members in the opposition vying also for power to rule the nation. However, our democracies in the world today are not the same as the kingdom of God. The kingdom that God allotted to His children is from above. The kingdom of God is diametrically opposed to the types of democratic governments we have today in the world. The governments on earth are voted into power by man. God's government, on the other hand is directed by God from heaven (theocracy). Instructions are given to man on how to rule the Earth and man is to follow them in detail as prescribed by God. Man is created in the divine family of God and his work is to carry onto completion what God has ordained from the beginning of creation. That was why God said, "Let Us make man in our image, after our likeness" (Gen. 1:26).

God, Jesus, and the Holy Spirit were present at the beginning of creation. Since man is created in the image of God, and also having His character (image), it means that there has to be a special relationship between God and man. God will give His directives and man's actions here on earth were to reflect the character that he was created for. However, man was made a living soul.

"And the Lord God formed man of the dust of the ground, and breathed into his nostrils the breath of life; and man became a living soul" (Gen. 2:7).

This means that God had not completed his work on man. His life was still conditional. If man abides by God's government, he will live forever. Being a living soul does not mean that man is an *immortal* soul. The word *soul* comes from the Hebrew word *nephesh* which means a breathing animal. All living creatures including animals were called *nephesh*. It is translated into English as *creature.* This means that man could still die. In Ezekiel 18:20, we read that, "The soul that sinneth, it shall die..."

The soul can decompose and die if it is not dependent on God's government. That is why the apostle Paul said, "The first man Adam was made a living soul; the last Adam was made a quickening spirit" (1 Cor. 15:45).

THE ENTERING OF SATAN INTO THE SCENE

This new form of government between God and man was looked upon with jealousy. God gave man the freedom of choice to do whatever he wanted. This is evident in Genesis 2 when God instructed man on what to eat and what not to eat. Man had the freedom to obey God or not. Man was not made as an automated machine. Even in our walk with God today, God does not deprive us from what we want to do. The choice is ours. God gave to man enormous power and numerous gifts to rule the world and live happily. The life accorded to man was eternal, so long as he obeyed and respected that relationship between him and God.

In the Garden of Eden, there was, *"The fruit of the tree of life"*, which man was to eat and live forever or, *"The fruit of the tree of the knowledge of good and evil"*. God forbade man from eating the fruit of the tree of the knowledge of good and evil because the day he eats it, he shall die. Many people view the fruit of the tree of life as God offering life to the world in His Son Jesus Christ. This life is eternal. It is God's nature and His uncreated life. The tree of life produces spiritual life while the other produces a soulish life. If man accepts the tree of life, he will become a spiritual being, and will become a partaker of the divine nature, or contrariwise, he will become soulish and embrace death to his own nature.

However, there was another creature who was opposed to this type of relationship between God and man. This was Satan himself. He has been with God from the beginning. He held a high position in heaven and he knew very well how the affairs in heaven and Earth were to operate. He wanted to make sure that the plan of God was thwarted. Everything that God plans to do for mankind, Satan is there developing a strategy to counteract every move by God. Satan wants man to understand that he is in charge, and not God. Satan wants man to believe in him, honor him, and follow his directions. Satan now came to Eve with a question. When Eve ventured to answer the question, she opened the door for Satan to come in. It would have been her place to rebuff Satan's question rather than enter into a conversation. That is the error that most Christians make today. We cannot outwit the devil; he knows us and our weaknesses. With this weakness of Eve, Satan now was encouraged to changed God's plan by suggesting to her that by eating the fruit of the tree of knowledge of good and evil, she will become like God – knowing good and evil.

"And when the woman saw that the tree was good for food and that it was pleasant to the eyes, and a tree to be desired to make one wise, she took of the fruit thereof, and did eat, and gave also unto her husband with her; and he did eat" (Gen. 3:6).

Satan took advantage of her weakness by entering into a conversation, and she fell into sin. Eve saw that, *"the tree was good for food"*, which we can equate today to, *"the lust of the flesh"*. It was good to the eyes, which is also, *"the lust of the eyes."*

With the fall of man, the flesh took over the Spirit. Their emotions and mind now governed their way of life. Adam and Eve rejected the truth and embraced unrighteousness. Adam knew that what he was eating was wrong in the eyes of God, but he still ate the fruit because of the affection he had for his wife. He wanted independence from God because, *"the fruit of the tree of life"*, made them dependent on God while, *"The fruit of the tree of the knowledge of good and evil"*, made them independent from God. Man could now strive for knowledge independent from God.

The fall of Adam and Eve was worse than a coup. Even when a coup takes place in a country by the military, there are some established systems in place, such as the ministers and the various workers. The ministers could be replaced, and some could be called by the coup plotters to continue with the new government. The president may be forced to resign or be overthrown militarily. The coup plotters may decide to execute some people summarily while others may be jailed.

However, what we are talking here is nothing to be compared to what man did by disobeying God. The disobedience of man was a revolt against God's established government. Disobedience allowed sin to creep into the world, which later led to disastrous consequences. Sin permeated to every aspect of life. It did not only sever man's relationship with God, but now everything God created was subject to decay and death. Man that lived with animals in the Garden of Eden, now became enemies. Animals started eating other animals. Man became an enemy to man. The rebellion ushered in racism, hatred, and bigotry in the world. God's original creation that was seen as *good,* now became marred with sin. God's original creation was a paradise on earth, and till today, we can still find traces of that paradise. The Scriptures declare in Psalms 19:1-3,

"The heavens declare the glory of God; and the firmament

sheweth his handiwork. Day unto day uttereth speech, and night unto night sheweth knowledge. There is no speech nor language, where their voice is not heard."

Since the fall, we still find traces of God's glory, and at the other end of the scale, we find evil, sorcery, and wickedness of the greatest proportion. Both man and animals prey on each other with impunity.

Today, we also find dictators all over the world who do not care about their subjects. What they care about are themselves and their families. We also find terrible situations where developed countries want to control all the resources of developing countries. They want to control the prices of commodities, even when they are not the producers themselves. In some cases, developing countries have to obey with the barrel of the gun, or their governments are either punished or overthrown.

As history continues, one generation reaps what the other has sown. The world, which the Lord created for us to take care of, has now become a scene of dominance and rapacious exploitation. Humans no longer think about what they will leave for the future generation, but what they can get to satisfy their greed.

As Plantinga, Cornelius Jr. points out, *"Human life is not the way it should be,....The world's greatest thinkers often diagnose the human predicament and prescribe various remedies for it. They diagnose ignorance and prescribe education. They diagnose oppression and prescribe justice. They diagnose the conformism of 'bad faith' and prescribe the freedom of authentic choice."*

Christians, on the other hand, see the present predicament as due to the fall of man. After the fall, man became a god to himself. He decides what to do, when to do it, and cares nothing about the consequences. Pride has eaten man as a cankerworm. Man has rejected God since the fall of Adam and Eve, and all we care about are ourselves, as we read in Genesis 3. Man heeded to Satan, and wanted to be *"like God knowing good and evil"*. This self-centered attitude has led to the forces of evil to grow even stronger in our society. Sin has violated the law, and drawn man further from God. Sin has become much more like a kid playing with a toy. We have accepted it, nurtured it, and accepted it as a norm. Sin is a rejection of what God meant this life to be. The moral standard laid by God has been corrupted by the fall of Adam and Eve.

Intellectually, higher education has complicated issues by rejecting the Scriptures, and has turned towards materialism. In the words of Herbert W. Armstrong, *"Education in the civilized world has become entirely materialistic, it has become a combination of the agnosticism of evolution, the politics and economics of Karl Marx, and the morals and social patterns of Sigmund Freud. Higher Education remains in utter ignorance of the mystery of mankind and of human civilization."* The rationalistic mentality that emanated from Europe has now become the norm in explaining our own evil, and running away from the truth. It is based on *"might is right"*.

Our society has become bankrupt with all sorts of evil, and every generation thinks that this is a form of civilization which should be emulated world-wide. Paul in Romans 1:18-32 outlines some of the problems we face in our society today, and he warns of the coming wrath that humanity is going to face because of sin. It is important we study some of these, and ask ourselves where we stand.

There is a righteousness from God that we believers must be conformed to, or we will face the wrath of God. This means that we are totally on God's side or we are against Him. There is no room for compromise. God's wrath is divine and not human. God's wrath is not intended to harm one another; it is His displeasure against sin. Whereas we are guilty sinners from birth, it is necessary we have a righteousness that we are blessed before God. That righteousness is only brought into the fore by our Lord Jesus Christ. It is not from our own works (Eph. 2:8-10). It is a faith whereby we are dependent on God.

God has revealed Himself to humanity, and any question about His existence, just portrays the stubbornness of man. Through nature, God has revealed Himself to us from this visible world to the invisible. Unfortunately, man has debased himself to the level of worshipping idols and other animals rather than the Creator.

It is for this reason that God has withdrawn from the sinner. Since people prefer sin rather than the righteousness that has been revealed, God has handed them over to their own lusts. People have given themselves to homosexuality, where men have sexual relationship with other men, and women having sex with other women. Sex in itself is good. It is meant for pleasure and progeny, but when people have a burning desire with people of the same sex, that is a curse! Such indecent acts always have their due penalty. When we reject the truth, there is a mark that follows it. When we turn away from God, we no longer think correctly, and as a result, the moral world in which we live is not properly understood.

Since these people claim that God was unnecessary, He gave them over to a reprobate mind, so that they are now doing what they were not supposed to do. The apostle Paul lists the number of sins from verse 29-32, and they are as follows:

"Being filled with all unrighteousness, fornication, wickedness, covetousness, maliciousness, full of envy, murder, debate, deceit, malignity, whisperers, backsliders, haters of God, despiteful, proud, inventors of evil things, disobedient to parents, without understanding, covenant breakers, without natural affection, implacable, unmerciful: Who knowing the judgement of God, that they which commit such things are worthy of death, not only do the same, but have pleasure in them that do them."

SPIRIT, SOUL AND BODY

Although people generally believe that a human being is generally dualistic, and is made up of a soul and body, it should be noted that such a belief is faulty and it is inconsistent with the teachings of the Bible. Although it is true that the soul is the invisible part, and the body is the visible part of the body, the Bible makes it clear that the physical being is made up of the spirit, soul, and body, and they are generally distinct from each other. A cursory look at 1 Thessalonians 5:23 reads as follows: *"And the very God of peace sanctify you wholly; and I pray God your whole spirit and soul and body be preserved blameless unto the coming of our Lord Jesus Christ"*. This verse shows that man is made up of a tripartite distinction of spirit, soul, and body. For a true Christian to operate well in the spirit, he should know these distinctions. Failure to understand them may lead to severe consequences, as we grow into spiritual maturity. Christians sometimes make errors in projecting their soulish life rather than their spiritual life. For us to attain that spiritual life, we must have a good grasp of spiritual knowledge. It is when we attain that spiritual knowledge, that we will be able to know the difference between our spirit and our soul. In order to attain that spiritual knowledge of God, we have to also humble ourselves to the Word of God. It has to be part of our being. It has to control us. It has to play an important part in taking care of our conscience and our intuitions. Such believers will have the knowledge and the experiences.

When Adam was created, prior to his fall, he lived by the breath of life, which became a spirit. He communed with God; he knew God's voice, and had a special relationship with God. After the fall, that special relationship with God was marred by sin. He was forewarned by the Lord that the day he ate, *"The fruit of the tree of good and evil, he shall surely die." (Gen. 2:17)*. Did Adam and Eve die instantly when they ate the fruit of good and evil? Absolutely not. After they were driven out of the Garden of Eden, they lived several hundreds of years. Then, what did God mean when he said that they shall surely die? God meant that Adam will be spiritually separated from God, but remain alive physically.

What therefore is death? The Webster's Universal dictionary defines death as, *"a permanent cessation of all vital organs: the end of life"*. Then what is spiritual death? Watchman Nee defines spiritual death as "the cessation of communication with God". Physical death is the cutting off of communication between spirit and body. Adam's spirit was dead because he could not communicate with God. The death that began from Adam and Eve soon spread from one generation to the other, and gradually merged with the soul, and they now became closely united. Since they have become one, it is the Word of God that can divide both of them, as we see in Hebrews 4:12:

"For the word of God is quick, and powerful, and sharper than any twoedged sword, piercing even to the dividing asunder of soul and spirit, and of the joints and marrow, and is a discerner of the thoughts and intents of the heart."

It is the Word of God that can divide the soul and spirit again, as it was before the fall of Adam and Eve, because since the soul and spirit are one, they plunge man into his own emotions and feelings because man no longer depends on God, but on self. The power of the spirit has been deadened, and man has no fellowship with God. The spirit is dead to God, but active to the things of the world. It is the flesh (the carnal mind) that is now in control. Even though man has contact with the spirit, this is total witchcraft, and has nothing to do with the Spirit of God. The body and the soul have now become one, and the Holy Spirit has no place to reside.

Jude 1:18 and 19 says;

"How that they told you there should be mockers in the last time, who should walk after their own ungodly lusts. These be they who separate themselves, sensual, having not the Spirit.

Our body, that was to relate to the Spirit, is now under the control of the soul. Man's spirit is under the control of the soul because the soul now dominates the body, and as a result, he is seen as a mocker, and pursuing his own passions in total rejection of God's government.

What then are the respective functions of the Spirit, soul, and body? It is through our body that we become conscious of our material world. The soul deals with our emotions or our intellect, which comes from our senses, and reveals our personality. It is linked to the spirit through the spiritual world and through the material world with our body. The soul stands between the spirit and the body. The soul is what Watchman Nee calls *"self-consciousness"*. It is through the spirit that we commune with God, and are able to worship and adore Him. With our spirit, we are God-conscious because it tells us about our relationship with Him. It is through our spirit that we can deal with the spiritual realm. The spirit can deal with the body through the soul. The spirit can subdue the body through the medium of the soul. Once the soul is subdued, it becomes easier to commune with God. The body can pull the spirit into loving the world. It is the soul that makes both the body and the spirit to communicate with each other, and it is the center of man's personality.

MAN AS THE TEMPLE OF GOD

As believers in Christ, we are the temple of God, because the spirit of God dwells in us. Whatever we do, we have to do it in the name of our Lord Jesus Christ. The apostle Paul wrote in his epistle,

"Know ye not that ye are the temple of God, and that the spirit of God dwelleth in you?" (1 Cor. 3:16).

As God was dwelling in the temple of old, we are God's temple of today, where the Holy Spirit dwells among the believers in Christ. In the Old Testament, the temple was divided into three parts,

a. The outer court where external worship was carried out.
b. The Holy place was where the priests entered and offered incense, oil, and bread to God. They are close to God, but they were not in the presence of God. They were still outside the veil and thereby could not stand in the presence of God.
c. The Holy of Holies was God's dwelling place, where no man can enter. It was foreshadowed by a brilliant light. The high priest was to enter only once a year, thus indicating that before the veil was rent, there can be no man in the Holy of Holies.

As believers in Christ, we are God's temple made up of three parts,

a. The body which is the outer court which is visible to all. It is visible in the broad day light. Man is obliged to obey the Commandment of God. Jesus died as a substitute for mankind.
b. The soul is the inner life of a man, which deals with our emotions, mind, and volition. It typifies a regenerated person who loves God. This represents the priests of the Old Testament.
c. The Holy of Holies is the secret place where no man has ever been. It is the secret place of the Most High. It is a place where God dwells. It cannot be reached by man unless God is prepared to rend the veil. This is man's spirit. It is here that man communes with God.

In the Holy of Holies, there is no light because God dwells there, just as we found in the Old Testament. The light is provided by a lampstand with seven branches. The spirit of man is like the Holy of Holies indwelt by God. In the Holy of Holies, we live by faith and not by sight. As the spirit communicates with the spiritual world, the body deals with the physical world, while the soul stands in between, and exercises its power to discern whether the spiritual or the natural should reign in the life of an individual. It should be noted that the spirit comes before the soul, and then the body. It is not the other way around. The reason is that the spirit is the most important part, then followed by the soul, and then the body.

All activities taking place in the temple of God, must be regulated by the Holy of Holies where God dwells. All activities in the outer court, must be regulated by the priests in the Holy place. Before the fall, man possessed the soul, but it was governed by the spirit. This is the order which God still maintains among believers today; spirit, then followed by the soul, and then the body.

REPENTANCE AND REGENERATION

After the fall of Adam and Eve, God did not give up on mankind, even though he was spiritually separated from Him. The sin of Adam and Eve brought severe consequences unto humanity till today. All humans are still facing the consequences of Adam and Eve eating the forbidden fruit.

As a result of the fall, God started to make covenants with man until Abraham. God told Abraham that he will be a father of many nations. Through Abraham, came the birth of Israel as a nation.

With the love God had for Israel, he delivered them from the hands of the Egyptians, and made a covenant with them at Sanai (The Sanaitic Covenant Exodus 19); and He gave them the Ten Commandments (Exodus 20:1-17). This Covenant was based on suzerainty. If they obeyed the covenant, they were blessed; if not, they will face severe consequences for breaking the law. At the same time, God also prepared a way for them, had they had sinned against Him. Any time Israel sinned, they were to acknowledge their transgressions, confess to the Lord, and amend their ways (Lev. 26:40b). They were to repent of all the offenses that they know, and then God will renew His Covenant with Israel (41-42). Moses, the servant of the Lord, also reiterated this point in

Deuteronomy 30:1-3; that if the children of Israel were to return to the Lord and obey Him, they will remain blessed. This is a clear theme of repentance. All Israel was to do was to repent and return to the Lord.

In the history of the Old Testament, any time Israel defected from the Lord, they were to return to the Lord with confession, obedience, and repentance of their sins. In some cases, repentance involved mourning, fasting, and prayers (1 Sam. 7:6). A soul that repents must have a change of heart and a rejection of sin. In Proverbs 28:13 and Psalms 32:3-5, repentance must begin by confession of known sins, and forsaking them.

If we study the life of Job, we learn that he was an upright man who suffered in the hands of Satan. He feared God above all else, but Satan persecuted him to test his faith. When God finally appeared to Job, he finally had a fuller knowledge of the Most High. He regretted about some of the careless words he spoke, and turned to the Lord and said,

"Wherefore I abhor myself, and repent in dust and ashes" (Job 42:6).

This therefore means that conversion and repentance lie with God, and that is why the psalmist said,

"Turn us, O God of our salvation, and cause thine anger toward us to cease" (Psalms 85:4).

In Psalms 51, a penitential psalm, King David cried out to God after his sin with Bathsheba. He did not hide his sin, but he poured out his heart in repentance. When Nathan the prophet confronted King David, he outlined all what he did in secret without hiding any. David pleaded with God to "cleanse" him and "blot" out all his transgressions.

In the New Testament, the first person to make this pronouncement was John the Baptist.

"Repent ye for the kingdom of God is at hand" (Matt. 3:2).

The necessary first step of salvation is *repentance* toward our Lord Jesus Christ. In Mark's gospel,

"John did baptize in the wilderness, and preach the baptism of repentance for the remission of sins" (Mark 1:4).

The apostle Peter reiterated this same point when preaching the gospel at Pentecost, when he said,

"Therefore let all the house of Israel know assuredly, that God hath made that same Jesus, whom ye have crucified, both Lord and Christ. Now when they heard this, they were pricked in their heart, and said unto Peter and to the rest of the apostles, Men and brethren, what shall we do? Then Peter said unto them, Repent, and be baptized every one of you in the name of Jesus Christ for the remission of sins, and ye shall receive the gift of the Holy Ghost." (Acts 2:36-38).

Here we find the word repent used in the imperative. We are being commanded by both John the Baptist and the apostle Peter in the Scriptures. Peter gave the conditions: we are to repent and be baptized. To those whom the Holy Spirit resides, belong to Christ (Rom. 8:9).

What then is repentance and what is it not? According to Proverbs 28:13, we learn that we cannot cover up our sinful life without confessing them, and also to make sure that we do not make it a habit of repeating them.

"He that covereth his sins shall not prosper: but whoso confesseth and forsaketh them shall have mercy." (Proverbs 28:13)

To repent means to be sorrowful and regret what you have done, or repent, which means here to breathe deeply.

Repentance is not feeling guilty of what you have done. The unbelievers also feel guilty for their actions. To repent means that you first acknowledge your sin, and then you repent to the Lord. In Acts 24:25, the apostle Paul was defending himself before Felix and Ananias, the high priest; "And as he reasoned of righteousness, temperance, and judgement to come, Felix trembled, and answered, Go thy way for this time; when I have a convenient season, I will call for thee."

Felix knew the truth, but he was not ready to repent. This is typical of unbelievers who feel guilty of something, but they are not prepared to repent.

It may sometimes happen that you may be remorseful of an action that you have taken. This does not mean that you have repented of that particular action. Even if you are remorseful of your decision, as a Christian, you need to repent to God. "For godly sorrow worketh repentance to salvation not to be repented of: but the sorrow of the world worketh death" (2 Cor. 7:10).

Sometimes we think that being exceptionally good leads to repentance. There are some people who are naturally good in character. You may sometimes think that they are Christians when they are really not. Having an exceptional character does not make you righteous before God. Prophet Isaiah has this to say; "But we are all as an unclean thing, and all our righteousnesses are as filthy rags; and we do all fade as a leaf; and our iniquities, like the wind, have taken us away" (Isa. 64:6).

Our self-righteousnesses are as *"filthy rags"*. Isaiah the prophet refers to the menstrual cloth which was used during a woman's period to picture uncleanness (Lev. 15:19-24). How terrible sin looks! It is nasty and ugly.

Repentance does not entail being religious. It is only true repentance that will lead us into salvation. The Pharisees and Sadducees were very religious people. The Pharisees fasted and prayed for hours. They were a legalistic sect of the Jews who were known for their strict adherence to the law. Jesus always rebuked them for using human tradition and for their hypocrisy (Matthew 15:3-9). They made sure that they practiced all religious ceremonies, yet they never repented. When the

Sadducees came to where John the Baptist was baptizing, he said to them,

"O generation of vipers, who hath warned you to flee from the wrath to come? Bring forth therefore fruits meet for repentance" (Matt. 3:7-8).

This was a sect that accepted only the books of Genesis to Deuteronomy. They also rejected the supernatural, including the raising of the dead and the existence of angels. That is why they were rebuked by John the Baptist for their ritualistic and naturalistic beliefs.

Repentance does not mean that we know the truth. We can attain academic excellence and acquire knowledge concerning this life. However, this does not mean that the truth has become a living reality. Rationalism has become a part of thinking, and we have deviated from the Bible, which is the living truth about life.

What then is Repentance? It is when you are sorrowful to God, and feel guilty for what you have done. You acknowledge the fact that you have sinned first against God, and then to your fellow man. It is a condition of being truly converted by receiving the Holy Spirit. As a new convert, whatever you have in mind which you cherish so much, must be destroyed and you must allow the Holy Spirit to make a residency in your mind and take control of all your self-centeredness. All aspects of your life that does not glorify God must be destroyed. You must accept your own emptiness and embrace God's greatness in your life. You have to be brought to a point where you feel you are nothing, you are worthless, and you are terribly sorry for your sins. This is deep repentance before God. Deep repentance means God's thoughts have to take over your own thoughts. This is a total surrender to God.

A good example is Psalms 49, 50, and 51, which King David composed when Nathan the prophet exposed his sin against Bathsheba. David was a man who had a weakness when it concerned women. It happened that Bathsheba, the wife of Uriah, was bathing naked when David spotted her. That night, the king could not sleep. His heart burned within him with the desire to have her to satisfy his own cravings-a desire that will torment him all the days of his life. What he did against Bathsheba tormented him and all Israel all the days of his life. What a tragedy for a king to go so low.

Bathsheba got pregnant and King David thought he could easily do away with it without anyone knowing. He sent a message to Uriah to come home to be with his wife while the other soldiers were at the war front. The king wanted Uriah to sleep with his wife, but he did not cooperate. His plans to get him drunk so that he could sleep with his wife did not also workout as he thought.

As his plans did not work, he sent a letter to Uriah's commander to put him at the war front so that he could be easily killed and his sin could be covered up. King David's plan worked this time, but could he go away with it? Everything looked normal in the beginning, but for how long? That was when the Lord sent Nathan the prophet to expose his sin. Nathan said to the king, "There were two men in one city, the one rich, and the other poor" (II Samuel 12:1).

Nathan the prophet now started unfolding the story to the king. The story rankled King David's emotions and he was very angry against the man and he said to Nathan, "As the Lord liveth, the man that hath done this thing shall surely die" (verse 5).

King David did not realize that he was talking about himself and what he did to Uriah. At this point, Nathan said to the king, "You are the man" (verse 7). Wherefore hast thou despised the commandment of the Lord, to do evil in his sight?"

Nathan asked a hard question. "Thou has killed Uriah the Hittite with the sword, and hast taken his wife to be thy wife, and hast slain him with the sword of the children of Ammon" (verse 9).

Yes, King David orchestrated the act although he was not the one who carried out the act. God knew every detail in the heart of the king. King David thought that either God did not know or He must have forgotten the whole episode. What a lie! The child died and everybody knew about the story.

The sin of David stirred the heart of his son Absalom to overthrow him because he felt the father was unqualified to be king. The sword did not depart from the house of King David because he despised God. When King David realized his sin, he said, *"I have sinned against the Lord"* (verse 13). He did not say I have sinned against Uriah or Bathsheba.

Psalm 51 is very essential because it shows what true repentance is. This is where most of us really begin. However, if we look at psalms 49 and 50, we see that that is where King David started his repentance. He made a public proclamation to the whole world when he said, "Hear this, all ye people; give ear, all ye inhabitants of the world" (Psalm 49:1).

King David was here making a public proclamation of himself and in verse 4, the king said, "I will incline mine ear to a parable." He was talking about the parable Nathan the prophet told him. The following verse depicts his bemoaning his sin with Bathsheba. Despite the fact that he is a king and very rich, he cannot go away with it. He cannot redeem Uriah who is dead. He cannot give eternal life to anybody. When you sin, it hurts other people as well. Bathsheba's family was wrecked. He husband died in the war and she lost her son finally.

In psalm 50, despite the sacrifices King David was making, it meant nothing before the Lord because his sin was still holding him captive.

"I will not reprove thee for thy sacrifices or thy burnt offerings, to have been continually before me" (Psalm 50:8).

God was telling David that his gifts meant nothing to Him because all things belong to Him. Those sacrifices were just to point people to Christ's sacrifice. When you commit a sin, you ram up a spear into Christ's side. That is the reason He died with him

In verse 17, God reproves David of his sin by telling him, "Seeing thou hatest instruction, and castest my words behind thee."

David had forgotten his covenant with God so God was angry with him. In verses 18-20, God was now specific about the sins of David. "When thou sawest a thief, then thou consentedst with him, and hast been partakers with adulters. Thou givest thy mouth to evil, and thy tongue framest deceit. Thou sittest and speakest against thy brother; thou slenderest thy own mother's son."

David has now involved himself into thievery, adultery, murder, deceit, slander, lies telling etc. "These things hast thou done and I kept silence; thou thoughtest that I was altogether such an one as thyself: but I will reprove thee, and set them in order before thy eyes" (verse 21).

God had let nine months to pass before stepping into the scene to reprove David of his sins. God was giving David a chance to repent of his sins, but he was very stubborn and thought all was over. God does not remember it any more. As God was patient with David, so He is patient with us also. None of us is above the law. Everyone is subject to the law-that is why Christ died for our sins. A penalty must always be paid to the law. Psalm 50 shows how David is bitterly repentant. He was learning about repentance toward God. It hurts a father when a child commits sin. It is the same thing with God. We must always repent of what we have done wrong.

King David did not hide anything from God. He poured out his heart, and asked for forgiveness from God (Ps. 51:1-3). King David himself outlines the specific sins he committed, and did not hide anything from His Creator (vs. 3-4). King David showed a true attitude of contrition when he mentions *"a broken spirit"* and a broken and contrite heart" (v. 17). The king went further to ask the Lord to "purge him with *"Hyssop"* of all his iniquities (vs. 7-9). He was pleading with the Lord to *"cleanse"* and *"wash"* him, and to *"blot out all his iniquities."* He asked the Lord to *"create in me a new heart"*, and to *"renew a right spirit"* in him (v. 10). After falling from sin, King David asked the Lord to *"restore"* unto him the *" joy of "salvation""* (v. 12).

True Repentance means you have to be truthful about your sin, just as King David acknowledged his sin in psalms 51. In Psalms 32:5, the psalmist said, "I acknowledged my sin unto thee, and mine iniquity have I not hid. I said, I will confess my transgressions unto the Lord; and thou forgavest the iniquity of my sin."

This goes in line with what David said in Psalms 51:3.

Repentance also means turning away from your sins. As a child of God, we should do everything to avoid sin. It shouldn't be part of our nature. In Proverbs 28:13, King Solomon said, "He that covereth his sins shall not prosper: but whoso confesseth and forsaketh them shall have mercy."

Repentance involves paying back what you owe. We are not to keep any outstanding debt, without making an attempt to pay it back. That in itself is sin. Zacchaeus, who was a tax collector, made sure that he paid back what did not belong to him. "And Zacchaeus stood, and said unto the Lord; Behold, Lord, the half of my goods I give to the poor; and if I have taken anything from any man by false accusations, I restore him fourfold" (Luke 19:8).

REGENERATION

Since all humans are spiritually dead because of the fall of Adam and Eve, the only means of coming back to God, is through the process of repentance and regeneration. A spirit without repentance is far from God, and is dead because it is not under God's control, and has no way to commune with God. Due to the present predicament, man is under the control of his soul, and he can do whatever he chooses. It is his imagination that controls him.

When does regeneration come into the life of the believer? Does it come after repentance or regeneration? The truth of the matter is that repentance comes before regeneration. Repentance comes through the will of man, while regeneration is done by God Himself. While repentance takes a short period of time, regeneration takes a longer period because it affects your moral behavior over time. We all convert to become children of God, and from there, regeneration starts working in the life of the new believer. In John 1:12-13, we read,

"But as many as received him, to them gave he power to become the sons of God, even to them that believe on his name: Which were born, not of blood, nor of the will of the flesh, nor of the will of man, but of God."

To "receive him" means to acknowledge Jesus, and put our faith in Him that He is the Word of God. Verse 13 informs us about the divine side of salvation. It is not man to produce salvation, but God. Sinners, who convert to Christ, are regenerated beings. As human beings, we belong either to God or to Satan. If we are converted and regenerated, we become the children of God. If not, we are under the control of Satan. In order to better understand this process of regeneration, let us look at the conversation between Jesus and Nicodemus.

Nicodemus was a Jewish Rabbi, who came to Jesus by night to reason with Him about this new doctrine that He was preaching. In John 3:3, the first statement Jesus uttered was: "Verily, Verily I say unto thee, Except a man be born again, he cannot see the kingdom of God."

This was a Jewish Rabbi who understood Scripture; however, he was taken back by this statement. He never understood what the Lord was saying. This was the Good News rejected by the Pharisees and Sadducees. This was already mentioned in the book of Malachi 3:1,"Behold, I will send my messenger, and he shall prepare the way before me: and the Lord, whom ye seek, shall suddenly come to his temple, even the messenger of the covenant, whom ye delight in: behold, he shall come, saith the Lord of hosts."

This verse was quoted in Mark 1:2. It is after this that we find the account of John the Baptist to prepare the way before the messenger. The Jewish leaders never knew who this messenger was. They did not know that God has sent Jesus to declare the Kingdom of God.

We read further, and find that Nicodemus was confused. He did not understand what Jesus was talking about. "How can a man be born when he is old? can he enter the second time into his mother's womb, and be born?"

Jesus decided to simplify things for Nicodemus in verses 5-6. "Verily, verily I say unto thee, Except a man be born of water and of the Spirit, he cannot enter into the kingdom of God. That which is born of the flesh is flesh, and that which is born of the Spirit is spirit."

The Pharisees knew about water baptism. They had used it several years to convert Gentiles into Judaism. They were also conversant with the baptism of repentance by John the Baptist-a baptism of repentance "for the remission of sins" (Mark 1:4).

Jesus also said, "That which is born of the flesh is flesh, "Jesus is telling us that we are mortal beings composed of flesh and blood. "That which is born of the Spirit is spirit."

We are no longer flesh and blood, but IMMORTAL beings! Jesus continued His conversation with Nicodemus,"Marvel not that I said unto thee, Ye must be born again. The wind bloweth where it listeth, and thou heareth the sound thereof, but canst not tell whence it commeth, and whither it goeth: so is everyone that is born of the Spirit" (John 3:8).

Jesus is saying here that just as the wind cannot be controlled or understood by human beings, but we can feel its effect, it is exactly what happens with the Holy Spirit. You cannot see the wind. It is the same thing that you cannot see the Holy Spirit. You can only feel its effect in your life, just as you feel the wind. When the Holy Spirit is working in our life, there is apparent evidence, and can be proven in our daily walk with the Lord. It was rather unfortunate that Nicodemus, who was a Pharisee, could not understand. It is the same with some of our churches today. They do not yet understand what being BORN AGAIN means. They do not yet understand what the Kingdom of God is. As a born again Christian, the spirit's work of regeneration renews the heart, restoring us from the fall of Adam and Eve.

Hebert W. Armstrong gives a good illustration of a born again Christian. He pointed out that human life started with what is called a *"corruptible seed"*-physical male sperm. Once we are born again, we become incorruptible-the Holy Spirit now starts to work in our lives. Armstrong went further with his illustration, *"But as the human embryo must GROW till it becomes a fetus, which must GROW to the point of being born into the human family, so the Christian in whom divine life has been started by the gift of God's incorruptible Spirit must grow toward perfection to be born into the GOD family. He will then be perfect, unable to sin."*

The apostle Peter illustrated this in 1 Peter 1:23, "Being born again, not of corruptible seed, but of incorruptible, by the word of God, which liveth and abideth for ever."

Being represents a process that has begun. The born again Christian now becomes incorruptible by the Spirit of God within him. It continues throughout our human life, so long as we continue to abide in the Lord. It should be noted here that the Spirit of God is the incorruptible *"seed"*, which imparts eternal life in a believer.

In chapter 2:1-2, Peter continues his discussion about the

born again Christian. "Wherefore laying aside all malice, and all guile, and hypocrisies, and envies, and all evil speakings, as new born babes, desire the sincere milk of the word, that ye may grow thereby:"

"Laying aside" and *"malice"* here means that we need to purge ourselves by renouncing all sins, so that the Word of God can have its residency in our lives. Armstrong refers to this as the *"gestation"* period to the growth of a new born human physical baby. Peter is here comparing a new born baby with a new Christian who needs to be nourished by the Word of God, so that the person can GROW. Just as new born babies must by nourished in order that they can grow, the new believer needs to also grow spiritually. We need the spiritual knowledge so that it can impact our character. It is at this level that we have a new life in Christ, which continues from God if we do not backslide. We learn how to serve and love God as we grow daily, by studying the Word of God. We can repent from time to time from known sins, although this should not be habitual, but we are born into spiritual life forever. As we continue in the Lord, outward appearances as a Christian will manifest. Others will see it. Your character will be changing gradually as you strive towards perfection, when you are born as a spirit being. This is because perfection cannot be attained here on earth. As Christians, we are still dependent on God, just as the new child is dependent on the parents. In 1 John 5:11-12, this is clearly brought forth, "And this is the record, that God has given to us eternal life, and this life is in his Son. He that hath the Son hath life: and he that hath not the Son of God hath not life." It is impossible for us to have this life without Christ. The very life we possess in Christ, is expressed in the grace and power that Christ provides all the time to His children. We are not independent of Christ. We are still dependent on Christ, as we are still here on earth.

Armstrong went further to compare a born again Christian

and a new born baby, *"A born human baby has human life on its own-independent of its mother. THAT DEFINES THE STATE OF BEGETTAL AND A BORN STATE! The only difference is, in the Christian life we are fed and protected by and through the spiritual mother-the church, while our actual eternal life comes to us through and from God. But when BORN again of GOD, we shall have ETERNAL LIFE INHERENT-of our own! We are NOT now in that state."*

SPRITUAL TRANSFORMATION

We have just completed the chapter on Repentance and Regeneration. This is a necessary first step in our walk with the Lord. The life we live should be a reflection of the Scriptures, for Christ Himself said: "If you love me, keep my commandments" (John 14:15). This therefore means that as believers, our life is dependent on God. We attend Bible study every week and church service every Sunday. We want to grow closer to God. If we care about our spiritual life, we need to care about where our spirit is leading us. This is because our mind is always in a constant spiritual battle. We fast, we pray, and we ask for God's guidance. Why should we spend our time seeking God's presence? The apostle Paul said in Galatians 5:16-17, "This I say then, Walk in the Spirit, and ye shall not fulfill the lust of the flesh. For the flesh lusteth against the Spirit, and Spirit against the flesh: and these are contrary the one to the other: so that ye cannot do the things that ye would."

Why will Paul say this? It is because of our human nature. Since the fall of Adam and Eve, we have developed our own values, and many of us have been holding on to it tenaciously, even when we profess that we are Christians. In certain cultures, especially in third world countries, we still believe in our ethnic values, and we think we can live alongside with it as Christians. When I was working as a research linguist and literacy consultant with Wycliffe Africa, I met a woman who was a translation consultant among the Mambillas in northern Cameroon. She was telling some members of another translation team that when the translation team was translating Paul's writings concerning immorality, natives cried out and said immorality was part of their culture. When the consultant told them that that is what God wants them to do by fleeing fornication, they said it will cause a problem in their culture. The translation consultant told them that that is what God is demanding from them because it is from the Word of God. It caused so much confusion even among the local pastors from that area. Finally, they had to choose either to abide by the Word of God or to abide by their culture.

In the western culture, we are faced with legal, political, religious, scientific, artistic, and academic viewpoints. Academics has shaped the minds of people in the Western world. There are those who believe in Darwinism, even though they cannot prove the theory of evolution from Scriptures. Charles Darwin believed that there is a continuity between animals and man, which completely negates the concept of special creation by God. Darwin completely rejects the special creation of man by God through his brain, his speech, his memory, his conscience, his concept of God, and the soul. The Bible has proof about the existence of God. It is sad that in some Bible colleges and seminaries, some pastors have developed a doctrine that fits their denomination. Some of these Bible colleges have deviated from the truth in the Bible, and are more interested in history, human reasoning, and different cultures. Very little is taught from the Bible. Some of these institutions are more interested in high accreditation than training people in the fear of the Lord, and how to spread the good news. They have twisted the Scriptures to satisfy their congregational needs. Liberation theology, which emerged from Latin America under a Roman Catholic Peruvian, Gustavo Gutierrez, and others such as Robert Shaull and Rubem Alves, was aimed at liberating the oppressed. They believed that theology must start as a commitment of liberating the poor. It is a theology that has grown out of the human situation in history, rather than out of thought. According to them, as Cairns puts it, *"salvation is economic, social, political liberation from all sorts of oppression."* This theology completely negates what Christ teaches concerning the poor. Christ knew that we shall always have the poor among us, and it is our duty to take care of them. It is not our duty to introduce communist ideology and infuse it into Christianity.

From an academic world view, there are those who refuse the idea of human nature. If human nature is rejected, then how do we have the will to choose what is good and what is evil? The apostle Paul pointed out the works of the flesh (human nature) in Galatians 5:19-21

"Now the works of the flesh are manifest, which are these; Adultery, fornication, uncleanness, lasciviousness, idolatry, witchcraft, hatred, variance, emulations, wrath, strife, seditions, heresies, envyings, murder, drunkenness, revellings, and such like: of the which I tell you before, as I have also told you in time past, that they which do such things shall not inherit the kingdom of God"

Paul is pointing out life after the fall. It is important that we know what these words really mean to us as Christians. We were by nature in total control of the devil, and we were practicing the sin nature before we were taught how to be good Christians. As children of God, we are to avoid the works of the flesh. By our own power, we cannot overcome the sin (human) nature easily. We have to seek God in prayers, fasting, meditation, and in the study of God's Word. This is because even after we are converted, we can still be *"carnally minded"*. It is a deadly weapon that still remains within us as Christians, and we need to fight the good fight of faith through the power of the Holy Spirit, to overcome it. We will here deal with the meaning of those words spelled out by the apostle Paul.

THE WORKS OF THE FLESH

ADULTERY-It is sexual activity or intercourse outside the marriage union. Taking pleasure in pornography is also part of it (Exod. 20:14; 1 Cor. 5:1).

FORNICATION-The Webster dictionary defines fornication as consensual sexual intercourse between two persons not married to each other (Eph. 5:3; Col. 3:5).

UNCLEANNESS- or **LASCIVIOUSNESS**-It is following one's passions and desires to the point of having no shame or public decency (2 Cor. 12:21).

IDOLATRY-It is the worship of graven images, spirits; putting your trust in persons or admiring things from other people to the extent that you are having a passion to have it, which now becomes a sort of competition (Col. 3:5).

WITCHCRAFT-It involves worshipping of the dead, black magic, worship of demons, and the use of drugs to produce "spiritual" experiences (Exod. 7:11, 22; 8:18; Rev. 9:21).

HATRED-It is having an extreme dislike or enmity toward somebody.

VARIANCE-It is struggling for superiority, quarrelling, and antagonism toward one another (Rom. 1:29; 1 Cor. 1:11; 3:3).

EMULATIONS-It is being resentful or jealous against someone's success.

WRATH-It is extreme anger that leads to explosive words or deeds (Col. 3:8).

STRIFE-It is an unrighteous means of seeking for power or contending for superiority which sometimes can lead to conflict (2 Cor. 12:20; Phil. 1:16-17).

SEDITIONS-It is introducing divisiveness or division among people (Rom. 16:17).

HERESIES-It is creating divisiveness within members of the congregation, or presenting teachings in the church that are not supported from the Bible (1 Cor. 11:19).

ENVYINGS-It is having a dislike against somebody who has something that we desire (Rom. 13:13; 1 Cor. 3:3).

DRUNKENNESS-It is drinking excessively, which sometimes may affect your health.

REVELLINGS-It is excessive feasting or partying, which may lead to drugs, sex, alcohol, etc.

The apostle Paul made it emphatically clear that those who are engaged in such activities enumerated above, are shutting themselves from the kingdom of God, because these sins characterize those who are unredeemed and are living under the law. Although the sins enumerated above are not exhaustive in Galatians, they, however, cover three areas of human life: sex, religion, and human relationships.

THE FRUIT OF THE SPIRIT

Contrary to the sinful nature is the, "Fruit of the Spirit". This is what children of God should be striving for. We should all be striving for a godly attitude, as we are in an open warfare with the flesh. The Spirit produces fruit, which are nine in all, and they are inextricably linked to each other. "But the Fruit of the Spirit is love, peace, joy, longsuffering, gentleness, goodness, faith, meekness, temperance: against such there is no law" (Gal 5:22-23).

This is produced in the life of a believer who turns to God and wants to serve the Lord fervently. They allow the Fruit of the Spirit to take control of their lives, so that they can fellowship with their Creator. We shall take an in-depth study of these words in order to understand them deeply.

LOVE-The Greek word for love is *agape.* It is love that does not refer to emotional affection or physical attraction. It is a love that has a caring heart about other people without any particular motive (Rom. 5:5; 1 Cor. 13; Eph. 5:2). Love is supposed to be the paramount virtue of a Christian because it characterizes God. It is that love that led God to create humans. If this love is central to God's character, it should be central to us Christians also.

It is unfortunate that it is used loosely today. We love so many things around us, but they cannot measure up to the love of God for humanity.

JOY-It is experiencing happiness that comes from God's grace, blessings, and promises. It is based on spiritual promises that are eternal, and the believer knowing that he is right with God. The joy in the Lord can even be present when you are in very difficult circumstances, but still being dependent on God, and feeling happy with Him because of the blessings they already possess. (Psalms 119:16; 2 Cor. 6:13; 1Pet, 1:8; John 16:20-22; Rom. 14:17 etc.). Joy in the Lord is different from happiness (Psalms 4:7). When one has joy in the Lord, it means that you know and trust God, even in difficult circumstances, but happiness is a result of pleasant circumstances, such as having a good paying job, or a happy marriage, etc.

PEACE-It comes from God as we depend on Him, and believe in all that He has assured us here on earth. Even in cases of crises, we are still depending on Him. The peace of God does not depend on your circumstances; you accept graciously your situation even at the point of death (Rom. 15:33; Phil. 4:7; 1 Thess. 5:23; Heb. 13:20; John 14:27; Rom. 8:28; Phil. 4:6). Christians must pray for the peace of God to reign in their hearts, for Christ Himself said; "Peace I leave with you, my peace I give unto you: not as the world giveth, give I unto you. Let not your heart be troubled, neither let it be afraid" (John 14:27).

If there is partisan bickering and hatred for one another in the church, our homes, or our jobs, the peace of God cannot dwell with us. Our peace should be the one Jesus won on the cross. The peace of God comes into our heart when we cooperate with the Holy Spirit.

LONGSUFFERING-When we are faced with a difficult circumstance, we keep our emotions under control and become patient in difficult times, and slow to anger when we are inflicted by others (Eph. 4:2; 2 Tim. 3:10; Heb. 12:1). A person in such situations is always patient, mild, and gentle in those circumstances. We can see how God was patient with the city of Nineveh (Jonah 4:2). A longsuffering person is not derailed by his circumstances. He is constantly waiting on God to act or give him directions on what to do next.

GENTLENESS-It is better translated to be meekness. It is the ability to show kindness, and trying to submit to anyone's feelings. It is not aimed at revenging when someone hurts your feelings (Eph. 4:32; Col. 3:12; 1 Pet. 2:3).

GOODNESS-It is hating all that is evil, and loving that which is right in the presence of the Almighty God. It is moral and spiritual excellence manifested in times of crises (Luke 7:37-50; Rom. 5:7). Goodness expresses itself in good character; it is holiness put into practice. Goodness can only be predicated on God alone. There are good people around, but it is God that is good (Mark 10:18). Only God's goodness is absolute. All other goodness is only measured against this absolute standard.

FAITH-It is the inner peace which the believer possesses. It is believing in God and holding steadfastly to what He has promised to His children. It is the confident relationship one has with Christ (Matt. 23:23; Rom. 3:3; 1 Tim. 6:12; 2 Tim. 2:2; etc.).

Faith is an undeniable power we have from God, to the extent that we believe in an unseen reality. It is an undeniable power that comes from God. The writer in Hebrew 11: 1 says;

"Now faith is the substance of things hoped for, the evidence of things not seen."

MEEKNESS-It describes a person who is submissive to the Holy Spirit. It means to be humble towards God. The person is also very gentle, just as Moses in the Bible (Num. 12:3; Exod. 32:19-20).

It will also be necessary for us to distinguish meekness from weakness. Weakness comes as a result of negative circumstances that come our way, such as lack of courage or lack of strength. However, meekness is a conscious choice where our trust is in God. Jesus Himself said; "Take my yoke upon you, and learn of me; for I am meek and lowly in heart: and ye shall find rest unto your souls. For my yoke is easy, and my burden is light" (Matt. 11:29-30).

As children of God, we lean on Jesus, as opposed to pushing one's own ways. Meekness arises from strength, and not from weakness. We do not propagate our own assertiveness or self-interest. It comes from our trusting in God, and allowing Him to take control of our situation. "Blessed are the meek: for they shall inherit the earth" (Matt 5:5).

TEMPERANCE-It is controlling one's desires or passions (1 Cor. 9:25; 2 Pet. 1:5-6).

When a Christian is filled with the fruit of the Spirit, he does not need any law to change his behavior in order to please God (cf. Rom 8:4). There is no law that will hold back these Christian qualities. Temperance helps in maturing other Fruit of the Spirit.

The apostle Paul rounded up the Fruit of the Spirit by saying; "And they that are Christ's have crucified the flesh with the affections and lusts" (Gal. 5:24).

Children of God, who are prepared to follow the teachings of the Bible and abide by them through the power of the Holy Spirit, will always do what is good and right in the eyes of God. The Holy Spirit will always direct them to the right things, and lead them to avoid what is evil. This does not mean that the Christian has become totally perfect. The apostle John said; "If we say that we have no sin, we deceive ourselves, and the truth is not in us. If we confess our sins, he is faithful and just to forgive us our sins, and to cleanse us from all unrighteousness" (1 John 1:8-9).

John is making the point that the sinful nature is still present with us. It is a constant threat to believers, and we have to crucify the flesh through the power of the Holy Spirit. Once we commit a sin, we are to admit it, confess it, and seek forgiveness from God.

OTHER FRUIT OF THE SPIRIT

As children of God, we are to seek first the Spirit before anything else. It is after that that we can obtain whatever God has to offer us. However, these are not the only fruit of the Spirit. The question that will arise is, why then did Paul enumerate only what we have above? The answer is that Paul was dealing with his audience and knew exactly their challenges. There is no exact checklist concerning the Fruit of the Spirit. Many fruits of the Spirit are enumerated in 1 Timothy 6:11:

"But thou, O man of God, flee these things; and follow after righteousness, godliness, faith, love, patience, meekness."

"But thou hast fully known my doctrine, manner of life, purpose, faith, longsuffering, charity, patience" (2 Tim. 3:10).

"And beside this, giving all diligence, add to your faith virtue; and to virtue knowledge; And to knowledge temperance; and to temperance patience; and to patience, godliness; And to godliness brotherly kindness; and to brotherly kindness charity" (2 Pet. 1:5-7).

The apostle Paul echoed the qualities of love in 1 Corinthians 13:4-8, and stated that,

"Charity suffereth long, and is kind; charity envieth not; charity vauntheth not itself, is not puffed up. Does not behave itself unseemly, seeketh not her own, is not easily provoked, thinketh no evil; Rejoiceth not in iniquity, but rejoiceth in the truth; Beareth all things, believeth all things, hopeth all things, endureth all things. Charity never faileth: but whether there be prophecies, they shall fail; whether there be tongues, they shall cease; whether there be knowledge, it shall vanish away."

"Godliness", as mentioned in 1 Timothy 6:11, means reverence, respect, and piety toward God. In 2 Peter 1:5-7, we have the quality of *"virtue"*, which is not mentioned in Galatians 5:22-23. It means modesty and purity, and it is associated with godliness. This is indispensable in the Christian life.

Paul also offers us "hope" in Romans 5:4-5. Hope should be inherent in the Christian character. Our faith should be based on what we are expecting.

Peter also spoke of "knowledge". What does knowledge play in the life of a spirit-filled Christian? How does it relate to other gifts? It depicts who we are in Christ Jesus. How then does a spirit-filled Christian grow? As children of God, we cannot do anything on our own part, but the Holy Spirit in us can grow, when we submit to the Scriptures, as seen in John 15:8: "Herein is my Father glorified that ye bear much fruit; so shall ye be my disciples."

The growth of a Christian must be followed by the following qualities:

1. Through the study of the Word (2 Tim. 3:16).
2. Through prayer
3. Through our witness
4. Through meditation of the Scriptures.

TRANSFORMATION OF THE MIND

The mind is the center of our thought life. It is through our mind that we can know things by getting information, remembering things of the past, and understanding our environment. The center of our mind is the brain. It is through the brain that we reason and gain wisdom; and it is the center of our intellect. It is in our mind that we take decisions concerning our life and our future. Our mind is in constant battle when we are faced with a situation. It is through our mind that Satan easily creeps in, and sometimes holds us captive. Even the apostle Paul had this to say in 2 Corinthians 10:4-6; "For the weapons of our warfare are not carnal, but mighty through God to the pulling down of strong holds; Casting down imaginations, and every high thing that exalteth itself against the knowledge of God, and bringing into captivity every thought to the obedience of Christ."

The Christian is in a constant spiritual battle, and the apostle Paul tells where the battle begins. It begins in our mind. We need to wage war against our mind being held captive by the enemy. We need our minds to be in total harmony with that of Christ, and not the other way around. Prior to regeneration, "The god of this world hath blinded the minds of them which believe not, lest the light of the glorious gospel of Christ, who is the image of God, should shine unto them" (2 Cor. 4:4).

Satan holds our mind, and makes it blind to the reality of things. Man's mind has been so darkened that the light of the gospel has made them unwise, and rendered them as fools, even though they claim to be wise. Their mind becomes *"hardened"* to the truth of the gospel, and as a result, they fall back to their own desires, and it makes them hostile to the things of God. The mind is imprisoned by Satan, and it becomes the strong hold of Satan, where it transmits wicked thoughts, so that other men could also be held captive, and not submit to God.

It should be noted that even after repentance, it takes time for the mind to turn towards God, and that is why the apostle Paul wrote to the church in Corinth saying; "But I fear, lest by any means, as the serpent beguiled Eve through his subtilty, so your minds should be corrupted from the simplicity that is in Christ" (2 Cor. 11:3).

Paul was afraid that the Christians in Corinth will derail from the truth, and be blinded by Satan, since he is the god of this world. It is through our mind, that Satan always carries the first attack, in order to draw us back from the simplicity of Christ. Let us not forget that Eve was without sin, but she was convinced by the thoughts of Satan, and she ate the fruit of the tree of good and evil. As children of God, we have to be alert and alive in the spirit, to repulse all the wicked thoughts that are coming to us. Every wicked decision is first formed in our mind. It is through the mind that Satan passes before affecting our body.

The apostle Paul wrote; "I beseech you therefore, brethren, by the mercies of God, that ye present your bodies a living sacrifice, holy, acceptable unto God, which is your reasonable service. And be not conformed to this world, but be ye transformed by the renewing of your mind, that ye may prove what is that good, and acceptable, and perfect, will of God" (Rom. 12:1-2).

In this present discourse, Paul is concluding his message from chapters 1-11 by the word "therefore", in which he discusses about God's mercy in bringing salvation to both Jews and Gentiles. Paul was totally moving away from the theology of God's redemption in Jesus Christ, to the practical life, which the Christians are supposed to live according to the Scriptures.

In Romans 12:1, Paul is exhorting, counseling, and pleading to the Christians by using the word *"beseech"*, so that they must respond by offering themselves to God.

"By the mercies of God", the apostle Paul is reminding the Christians about the grace which was expounded in the first eleven chapters, (1:6-7; 3:24; 5:2 etc.), righteousness (1:17; 3:21-22; 4:5-6; 5:17, etc.), and the gift of faith (1:5, 17; 3:22, 26; 4:5, 13; 5, etc.).

"That ye present your bodies a living sacrifice" means that because of God's mercies to us, believers should surrender their lives completely to the Lord. We have to yield all our members as instruments of righteousness. Paul uses the word "sacrifice" to remind the Jews of the Old Testament Law. God accepted the sacrifice of animals without blemish (defect). The shedding of blood by the offering of animal sacrifices was for the redemption of sin (Lev. 1:2, 11, 15; 8:15). It should be noted that *"without the shedding of blood, there is no remission"* of sin (Heb. 9:11-14, 19-22). Aaron and his children were in charge of the office of the High Priest, so that people could offer sacrifices. In the New Testament, Jesus became our Great High Priest, and offered Himself as the all-sufficient sacrifice for sin. That is why John the Baptist said, "Behold the Lamb of God, which taketh away the sin of the world" (John 1:29).

As believers in Christ, we have offered ourselves to God, and we are kings and priests (Rev. 1:6); we are set apart for God's work here on earth, and are now a holy nation (1 Pet. 2:9). We are to proclaim the gospel of salvation.

Paul uses the phrase, "reasonable service", to mean that we owe God the highest form of service. We are to serve God wholeheartedly, which is our priestly spiritual service, which was formerly an Old Testament part of worship.

"And be not conformed to this world". Paul implies several things here. As believers in Christ, there is the danger that we may sometimes face pressure to conform to the world system (1 John 2:15-16). True believers must resist pressure from the world. There is an imminent danger among Christians when they conform to an outward appearance, masquerade themselves, and are different within.

"But be ye transformed" means that there has to be a change in outward appearance, which is a reflection of the inward character. Transformation takes place when the Holy Spirit renews our mind, and we grow to become like Christ. The kingdom of Christ is not of this world (John 8:36). This world's kingdom is of full of deception, darkness, and seduction (Matt. 4:6; John 3:19; 1 Cor. 6:9-10). Believers in Christ should eschew evil, such as greed, self-centeredness, arrogance, pride, revenge, envy, hatred, lust, sexual immorality, ungodly entertainment, fashionable clothes that are immodest and sexually seductive, drugs, intoxication, worldly companions, unrighteousness, power grab, etc.

Transformation takes place when your lifestyle is under the control of the Holy Spirit. Our minds should be renewed daily. If our mind begins to drift away from God, it is there that we start moving away from God. The light of God begins to move toward the believer through the Word of God, and the divine Spirit begins to direct our will, to the extent that, at a certain point, our mind realigns itself with God and His ways.

This therefore means that we are sincerely seeking for God, since our mind is *"dead in trespasses and sins"*. We must do everything to retain God in our mind through the revelation of His Word.

What does the mind consist of? It consists of our memories, perceptions, and beliefs. Our mind is the basic source of our thinking; it relates to everything we do, evokes our thinking, and makes us what we are. It is through our mind that we develop ideas and different ways of interpreting things concerning this life.

As children of God, it is incumbent on our part to recognize the forces of evil that were controlling our mind when we were unbelievers, and what is to control our mind now as believers. The spiritual transformation of a believer is to replace what is evil with that which Jesus Christ has taught us from Scriptures. It is the only way to move from darkness into light. Colossians 1:13 says, "Who hath delivered us from the power of darkness, and hath translated us into the kingdom of his dear Son". Central to our redemption, is deliverance from the power of Satan, to the kingdom of our Lord Jesus Christ. The apostle Paul reiterated this point when he said in his epistle to the Philippians, "Let this mind be in you, which was also in Christ Jesus" (Phil. 2:5).

Christ's humility of heart and mind, should be found in us, His followers, who are called to be like Jesus. There is a song in the hymnal, which begins like this; *"Jesus loves me, this I know, for the Bible tells me so"*, is a good way of answering the devil, and putting him where he belongs. It should be noted that this process is gradual. Spiritual transformation does not come overnight. It helps in building our character in Christ over time.

In our earlier study, we learned that the fall of man came as a result of the disobedience of Adam and Eve. God's government was overthrown, and throughout history, we continue to find Satan at play in most human governments. Satan is constantly fighting to thwart all the plans of God concerning humanity. Thus, the difference between God and Satan are completely opposite to each other. God's ideas are different from Satan's ideas. Prophet Isaiah has this to say: "For my thoughts are not your thoughts, neither are your ways my ways, saith the Lord. For as the heavens are higher than the earth, so are my ways higher than your ways, and my thoughts than your thoughts" (Isa. 55:8-9).

The two ways between God and Satan are radically different, and as Christians, we have to strive to know God, with his ways and ideas, in His Word.

In Jesus's earthly ministry, He proclaimed God, and corrected the disinformation propagated by Satan. He proclaimed that those who believed in Him would have *"eternal life"*. Jesus also proclaimed the availability of the Kingdom of God by manifesting the power of God, in healing the sick, raising the dead, and by setting the captives free from demonic attacks of Satan. Prior to the end of Jesus' earthly ministry, Jesus said to His Father in prayer, "I have manifested thy power unto the men whom thou gavest me" (John 17:6).

In other words, He made the people to understand who God really is. For us to come closer to God, so that He should transform our mind, we have to love God passionately, and believe in Him. The apostle Paul has this to say;

"What shall we say then to these things? If God be for us, who can be against us? He that spared not his own Son, but delivered him up for us all, how shall he not with him also freely give us all things?" (Rom. 8:31-32).

God is prepared to forgive us, and we have our total security in Him. God's grace is showered on us, bringing salvation to completion

When Martin Luther was standing before his accusers at Worms, he said, *"Unless I am convicted by Scripture and plain reason-I do not accept the authority of popes and councils, for they have contradicted each other-my conscience is captive to the Word of God. I cannot and will not recant anything, for to go against conscience is neither right nor safe. God help me, Amen"*. The earliest printed version of his statement added the famous words: *"Here I stand, I cannot do otherwise"*. Christians are to apply their thinking to the Word of God, and meditate over it. Every decision we take in life should be directed by the Holy Spirit. The writer of Hebrews says; "Therefore we ought to give the more earnest heed to the things which we have heard, lest at any time we let them slip" (Heb. 2:1). Christians are not to be careless about their commitment to Jesus.

TRANSFORMATION OF THE BODY

So far, we have been discussing about the transformation of the mind. The mind is to conform to Christ's teachings in such a way that it has to manifest in our character. For this to take place, our body has to start rejecting the works of the flesh, and start entertaining the fruit of the Spirit. Our body has always been the center of focus when the mind takes a decision. When we yield to our mind, the body will portray whether what we are doing is good or evil. The body in itself is not evil, but it is the body that hinders people from doing what is right or wrong. The apostle Paul, when writing to the Romans, had this to say: "For that which I do I allow not: for what I would, that do I not; but what I hate, that do I" (Rom. 7:15).

You cannot attempt to obey the saving grace of our Lord Jesus Christ without obeying His commandments. Those who are in the world are controlled by their master Satan. Sin rules over them. It is when we are delivered from the power of sin that we are led by the Spirit of God. We are born in a world that fosters evil, and runs ahead of our plans. However, our body is not our own, and we need to care for it as servants of God. Paul had this to say to the church in Galatia, "I am crucified with Christ: nevertheless I live; yet not I, but Christ liveth in me: and the life which I now live in the flesh I live by the faith of the Son of God, who loved me, and gave himself for me" (Gal. 2:20).

Paul describes his relationship as a total reliance on Christ. If we say that we are Christ's, then our lives should be in total intimacy with our Lord Jesus Christ. As believers, we have been crucified with Christ, and we now belong to Christ. We are no longer our own. Because of salvation in Christ, sin no longer has control over us (Rom. 6:1). As such, our deeds and Words of our Lord Jesus Christ becomes a natural expression of who we are.

However, we must note that temptation will always come. Temptation resides nowhere but in our body. It is always there, and we can feel it when we reflect on what we are thinking. The apostle Paul made it clear: "Know ye not, that to whom ye yield yourselves servants to obey, his servants ye are to whom ye obey; whether of sin unto death, or of obedience unto righteousness?" (Rom. 6:16)

A believer in Christ is not supposed to allow sin to reign in his body. The spiritual battle among believers is, whether they will surrender to the sinful nature's inclinations, and then submit to sin's control, or will they yield to the Spirit's demands, and continue under Christ's dominion. This is a battle that is within Christians, and continues until they become spiritually mature in Christ. Paul reminded the Christians in Galatia; "For the flesh lusteth against the Spirit, and the Spirit against the flesh; and these are contrary the one to the other; so that ye cannot do the things that ye would" (Gal. 5:17).

What are those parts of the body that can easily entrap us? They are our eyes, feet, hands, and our tongue. These are the things that can set us up, and bring disaster to our lives.

Concerning the tongue, James has this to say; "And the tongue is a fire, a world of iniquity: so is the tongue among our members, that it defileth the whole body; and setteth on fire the course of nature; and it is set on fire of hell" (James 3:6).

There is an inclination to sin with our tongue, and this includes lying, exaggeration, teaching false doctrine, slandering, gossiping, boasting, etc. As mature believers, we are to guide our tongue, and subject it under the direction of the Holy Spirit. Since the tongue is a dangerous member of the body, James warns us in James 1:19,

"Wherefore, my beloved brethren, let every man be swift to hear, slow to speak, slow to wrath"

The tongue is a small member of the body, but it can defile the whole body, and even others. No one can *tame* it. Before physical violence erupts, there has to be verbal violence. When we lose our temper, it will manifest in our body, which shows that our inclinations are wrong.

What steps can we take to control our body? Dallas Williard points out some of the measures that we can take to control the whole body.

1. *We must actually release our body to God.* That is why Paul said in Romans 12:1:

> "I beseech you therefore, brethren, by the mercies of God, that ye present your bodies a living sacrifice, holy, acceptable unto God, which is your reasonable service."

We have to renew our body daily. We have to withdraw and meditate on the Word of God, and how it affects our lives. This should be done in a place where you are alone, and there is nothing to distract you.

2. *Do not idolize your body.* This means that your body should not be your ultimate concern. As you have totally surrendered to God, let it be controlled by Him, and not you anymore. You should not be worried about what will happen to you today or tomorrow. God is now in charge of you.
3. *Do not misuse your body.* It should not be used for sensual gratification, or to manipulate others. Bodily pleasure is not necessarily a bad thing, but when you become dependent on it, it becomes a bad thing. We also should not use our body to dominate or control others. Let us not use our body to elicit sexual thoughts and feelings to others. Let us allow our natural beauty to be in control of us, and not try to be sexy.
4. *The body is to be properly honored and cared for.* Our body is holy, and it must be properly noted that it belongs to God. The apostle Paul said,"Know ye not that your bodies are the members of Christ? Shall I then take the members of Christ, and make them members of an harlot? God forbid" (1 Cor. 6:15).

Since we have separated our bodies to God, they have to be properly cared for. They do not belong to us anymore. We need occasions when we have to be alone. We also need a time of rest. We should not wear out our body just because we are looking for money. We should take our Sabbath seriously! Sabbath is a genuine celebration of God in our lives. It is inseparable from worship. We need a solitary environment to allow our body to rest. This means lying on the floor or on a bed, and focusing on the things of God, and not on our personal worries.

Our body is meant to glorify God. The apostle Paul had this to say in 1 Corinthians 6:12:

"All things are lawful unto me, but all things are not expedient: all things are lawful for me, but I will not be brought under the power of any."

The verses following indicate the importance of the body. Paul is saying that by nature, all our natural affections, such as eating, drinking, and sex are natural and lawful (verse 13). Yet Paul says that they are not necessarily helpful, nor should they hold any one into bondage. We have to make a choice with our body for the glory of God. "Meats for the belly, and the belly for meats, but God shall destroy both it and them. Now the body is not for fornication, but for the Lord; and the Lord for the body (Verse 13).

The body is meant for food, but all foods are not necessary, since they are not eternal. A Christian is supposed to rise above the cravings of the body.

In the second part, it is noted that the body is not meant for immorality. We are the temple of the Holy Ghost, and we are no longer our own. The body is totally for the Lord. Immorality here does not only mean sex out of marriage; it also means indulgence within marriage as well. When we strive towards sanctification, we should understand that it includes the body as well. The life we live in the flesh should be distinct from that of the unbeliever, because we have been set apart for Christ. The body God has given to us is to be taken care of, and not to be used for personal gratification. We cannot say that we love God, and at the same time, we are practicing sin. Matthew 6:24 says; "No man can serve two masters: for either he will hate the one, and love the other; or else he will hold to the one, and despise the other. Ye cannot serve God and mammon."

Our bodies are the temple of the Holy Spirit, and we cannot soil it with the things of the world. The apostle Paul pointed this fact in 1 Corinthians 3:16-17: "Know ye not that ye are the temple of God, and that the Spirit of God dwelleth in you? If any man defile the temple of God, him shall God destroy; for the temple of God is holy, which temple ye are." Many Christians believe in the saving grace of the Lord, but they forget that their bodies are also important before God. If our bodies are totally surrendered to the Lord, the body will be delivered from sin, and God will heal us from our infirmities. A surrendered body will be a dwelling place for the Lord.

TRANSFORMATION OF OUR SOCIAL LIFE

What is our relationship with others? Are our closest friends children of God or are they unbelievers? The people we associate with, more often can tell us who we are. Amos 3:3 says, "Can two walk together, except they be agreed?"

If we say that we are children of God, then our friends should be those who will hate evil, and embrace Christ as their personal Savior. The apostle Paul reiterated this position when he wrote to the Corinthian church;

"Be not deceived: evil communications corrupt good manners" (1 Cor. 15:33).

This statement is true. The people you associate with will affect your conversation, and your entire body will be affected. If we say that we are children of God, then Christ is in control of our entire body. If we associate with unrighteous people, then, we are not heaven bound. The things we talk about are earthly and they do not glorify God. Our eternal security is found in Christ and not in man. In the New Testament, believers in Christ are called kings and priests (1 Pet. 2:9; Rev. 1:6). This means that we are separated for the kingdom of God. In the Old Testament, when Moses was consecrating the priests, he took a ram "And he slew it; and Moses took of the blood of it, and put it upon the tip of Aaron's right ear, and upon the thumb of his right hand, and upon the great toe of his right foot" (Lev. 8:23).

What does this mean? The blood put upon the right ear, is to help the priest to allow our spiritual ears to be open. We are to listen to God exclusively. We have to be very selective in our hearing and the people we deal with. The blood upon the right thumb is to allow us to handle only what pleases God, and not man. It also means our energy and power belongs to God. You have to use your strength to work for God. Your energy is not meant for worthless things that do not glorify God. The blood upon the great toe of the right foot is to let us understand that our feet are consecrated to walk close with our Lord Jesus Christ. You have to run and follow only God. Why are we priests? It is because God bought us, owns us, and has a legal right over us. Another reason is the love which He has for us. If God could not tolerate an animal without blemish, God will not tolerate believers in Christ who live a reckless life. Since Christ has consecrated us, we are to reject what is evil, and associate with what pleases God.

However, rejection of evil does not necessarily mean that things will be always pleasant. Turning to Christ sometimes leads to rejection in a community, friends, or family. I know of children of God who have been ostracized by their families because they have embraced Christ as their personal Savior. Some have backslidden and compromised with their families, while some have stood their ground and remained with the Lord. Those who have stood their ground have a promise from the Lord.

"And he shall turn the heart of the fathers to the children, and the heart of the children to their fathers, lest I come and smite the earth with a curse" (Malachi 4:6)

Some children who have stood their ground have been praying for their families, and in some cases, there have been great results. The miracles that God has done in the lives of their children have led to some of them also giving their lives to the Lord Jesus Christ. What a great victory! As children of God, we cannot live in an island alone. We need to associate with others. If you think that you can solve your problem alone, then your relationship with others will also be affected. It will affect your attitude, and people will recognize the change in behavior. Such an action is contrary to God's commandment; "By this shall all men know that ye are my disciples, if ye have love one to another" (John 13:35).

The love of God must dwell in our hearts. If Jesus loved us and gave Himself for us, we must also love one another. Failure not to love others as Christ has commanded us in His Word, means that we have rejected the eternal life promised us. "We know that we have passed from death unto life, because we love the brethren. He that loveth not his brother abideth in death" (1 John 3:14).

The life of every individual is intrinsically related to others. "God is love", the Bible says, and we are supposed to love one another. However, we should not compare the love of God with very shrewd people who only love for their selfish interest. They love because they are gaining something from you. If there is nothing to gain, their friendship ends immediately.

In our families, we may have difficulties relating with some members. When we are faced with such a situation, the tendency is for us to withdraw from such a bitter relationship, especially when we can identify what is causing the problem.

When we look at marriages today, we find that the divorce rate is very high. Why? It is because they did not know what it means to be married. Marriage is not just going to sign legal documents or blessing a marriage in the church. To be married is to give oneself to the other. Both partners want to make the relationship work. It is not one partner dictating to the other partner. It is both partners supporting each other physically, emotionally, and spiritually (Eph. 5:22-23). If the wife becomes pregnant, it is the responsibility of both the man and woman to take care of the blessing of the child. Once the child is born, the role of the father and the mother has to be complementary. It is not one partner abandoning the care of the child to the other. Tension at home should not be exposed to the child because it may have a negative effect in the child's upbringing.

In marriage, relationships must be "genuine" because the children will see how true the parents are with each other.

TRANSFORMATION IN THE CHURCH

If the children of God, who are members of the church, come together, then they will have choices to make. This is because the role of the church is to transform the lives of its members to conform to the image of our Lord Jesus Christ. This was the message Paul gave to the Colossian church when he said a church is,

"Where there is neither Jew nor Greek, circumcision nor uncircumcision, Barbarian, Scythian, bond nor free: but Christ is all, and in all" (Col. 3:11).

There is no distinction in the house of God. Christ is in total control of all spheres of life. The body of Christ is supposed to be united because we are all free from ethnic inclinations. The focus of the local assembly is Christ and Christ alone. As members of the Church, we have been called out by God to fulfill His mandate here on earth "And he gave some, apostles; and some, prophets; and some evangelists; and some pastors and teachers" (Eph. 4:11).

The whole purpose of these gifts is to equip the saints for the service of the Lord, and for building the body of Christ. Why is it so? It is "For the perfecting of the saints, for the work of the ministry, for the edifying of the body of Christ: Till we all come in the unity of the faith, and of the knowledge of the Son of God, unto a perfect man, unto the measure of the stature of the fullness of Christ" (Eph. 4:12-13).

There has to be oneness and unity among believers, if it is built on a sound biblical doctrine. It should not be built on the beliefs of the church which sometimes deviates from the truth. Believers in Christ are to possess a sound knowledge of Christ, which comes through prayer, faith, the study of the Word, and obedience to His Word. This does not mean that we do not have people who are spiritually weak and need help. In our journey with the Lord, we need help from one another. What we need in our local church is spelled out in Ephesians 4:17-6:24. It will be very necessary as Christians to spend some time, and to read carefully what the apostle Paul is talking about.

In our local churches, the leaders of the church and other members are to encourage members of their congregation, and also teach them the Scriptures. The leaders must also try to identify some of the flaws that are holding back some members of the congregation. When this is properly handled, we will begin to see spiritual transformation taking place in the life of a believer.

The apostle Paul wrote to the Church in Galatia; "Brethren, if any man be overtaken in a fault, ye which are spiritual, restore such an one in the spirit of meekness; considering thyself, lest thou also be tempted. Bear ye one another's burdens, and so fulfill the law of Christ" (Gal 6:1-2).

Paul is teaching us here that if we find others who are a moral failure, then those believers in Christ, who are spiritually mature, should help to restore such a person scripturally. To restore such a one means to perfect human character (2 Cor.:11), or to lead the person to true repentance, and to fulfill his commitment to Jesus Christ and His ways. When a person sins, there has to be a disciplinary action that has to be taken *"gradually"*. The person should be told his failure, and then encouraged to follow Christ as his personal Savior. No matter the situation, the person should be handled with the utmost care, and at the same time being firm concerning his sins. The basic process of restoration is outlined in Matthew 18:15-20. Here we find the prescription for church discipline. The goal of this process is to restore your brother or sister. In the process of restoration, it is imperative to tell the person his fault privately. If the person is recalcitrant, take a brother or sister, and approach the person again to point out his fault. If the person still refuses to repent, tell it to the church, so that the whole congregation will be aware of it. If the person is still unyielding, the person should be excommunicated and be regarded as a heathen. The reason for this is not to punish the person. It is to prevent him from polluting the church.

Restoring someone in a church does not mean that they are placed in a leadership or ministerial position. People who desire a leadership or ministerial position must meet the qualifications in 1 Timothy 3:1-7 or 4:1. Character issues are supreme in choosing leaders, and not the various gifts in the Spirit.

TRANSFORMATION OF THE SOUL

It will be quite superfluous for us to discuss again the causes of the fall of man, since it has already been covered in the first chapter. However, it is also important to note that the whole being of man and his relationship to God was marred because of the fall. The Spirit that had that dependent relationship with God was now replaced by the soul. Man wanted to be his own independent decision maker, and had the free will to do whatever he wants. The soul now directs man's life, and sin now took over man's life. The work of the soul is to now satisfy its master, Satan. This type of relationship between God and man was replaced by Satan and man. The sin nature now became a normal way of life. Whatever decision a man takes, it is the soul that energizes the individual. As Watchman Nee puts it, *"sin originates, soul executes."*

Once a new believer accepts Jesus Christ as His personal Savior, the spirit will start taking over the flesh gradually because the spirit is now quickened. The spirit and the flesh will start striving for authority over the whole man. As the believer grows, he will finally come to understand God's deliverance on the Cross of Calvary. He learns how to exercise faith in Christ. The old man now becomes crucified, and the person is now free from sin, which had rendered the body ineffective. With all lusts and passions behind him, he now moves into a new realm of life. At this point, the spirit has taken over the flesh, although he is still carnal.

The individual is still carnal because, although the body is dead to sin, the soul is still alive in his life. The sinful nature in the individual has been affected by the new life in Christ, but self-centeredness still persists in his life. His life at this time is still soulish. He is still guided by his own desires and inclinations, although the Holy Spirit is present in him.

As new born babies in Christ, the soul varies from one individual to the other, because we all have certain peculiarities that are inherent in us until we all go to eternity. If it were not so, life in heaven will be purposeless. As we grow into spiritual maturity, the believer has to deny himself, and carry the Cross.

"And he that taketh not his cross, and followeth after me, is not worthy of me. He that findeth his life shall lose it: and he that loseth his life for my sake shall find it" (Matt. 10:38-39).

Our faith must be exclusively in Christ. We must place our lives in Christ and nothing else. Every believer must totally surrender to the Lord Jesus Christ. When we surrender totally, the soul is denied its place in our life. That becomes the cross in our life.

As we become followers of Christ, there is always a price to pay. Once we follow the narrow path, the soul suffers terribly. That is how believers lose their life for the sake of Christ. We forsake the world and its ways, and follow Christ. We are to hate our natural ways, and yield ourselves to Christ and His ways. If our natural life does not diminish, it becomes an obstacle to our spiritual life. In Hebrew 4:12, we are instructed how to divide the soul and the spirit. The Word of God plunges in, and splits the soul and the spirit, and the soulish life can now be suppressed in the believer. The soul and the spirit are totally at war with each other. They are always fighting for mastery. "For the flesh lusteth against the Spirit, and the Spirit against the flesh: and these are contrary the one to the other: so that ye cannot do the things that ye would" (Gal. 5:17).

As children of God, we are to live according to the dictates of the Spirit. Our lives must be conformed to the death on the Cross. At this point, the soul has taken its proper position as it was in the Garden of Eden.

4

WISDOM

Mike Murdock says, "Wisdom is the master key to all treasures of life." I candidly believe in this statement because, just as King Solomon says it loud and clear in the book of Proverbs, "Wisdom is the principal thing; therefore get wisdom: and with all thy getting get understanding" (Prov. 4:7). It should be noted that the wisdom we are discussing here does not come from education, experiences, or age. The wisdom we are discussing here comes from God. The apostle Paul said, "Howbeit we speak wisdom among them that are perfect: yet not the wisdom of this world, nor of the princes of this world, that come to nought: But we speak the wisdom of God in a mystery, even the hidden wisdom, which God ordained before the world unto our glory" (1 Cor. 2:6-7).

We get the wisdom of God when we are saved. It has nothing to do with the wisdom of this world. Furthermore, God's wisdom leads sinners to the great sacrifice of history, in which Jesus Christ was offered on the Cross of Calvary, which paid the debt of our sins for all who believe in Him. This truth is revealed in the wisdom of the gospels in the New Testament, in which all believers will be saved. This is the *mystery* "which God had ordained before the world unto our glory."

Wisdom originated from God, and it ends only with God. The Holy Spirit distributes the wisdom of God to people who are searching for Him (1 Cor. 12:11). God also blesses His called ones with wisdom, according to their call in the ministry. "But every man hath his proper gift of God, one after this manner, and another after that" (1 Cor. 7:7). There are some individuals in the Bible whom God blessed with wisdom. They are as follows:

1. BEZALEEL

The Lord instructed Moses to build a Tabernacle (Exod. 25). Special instructions were given on how to build it. It was based on historical, spiritual, and typological significance. It was based on the stipulations given by the Lord Himself. It was to be the *sanctuary* (v 8), a place set apart for God to dwell, and also to meet His people. It was also *the tabernacle of testimony*, i.e., it contained the Ten Commandments, which was a reminder of God's holiness and our relationship with Him, which can never be separated so far as we continue to abide in Him. The tabernacle was also a place of forgiveness. It pointed to heaven, where there was a heavenly Tabernacle, and also to God, who was the final redemption when a new heaven and a new earth will come. Moses now had a huge task in his hands. For the tabernacle to be accomplished, people with special skills were needed. The Lord then directed Moses to a man called Bezaleel, and the Lord said, "And I have filled him with the spirit of God, in wisdom, and in understanding, and in knowledge, and in all manner of workmanship. To devise cunning works, to work in gold, and in silver, and in brass, And in cutting of stones, to set them, and in carving of timber, to work in all manner of workmanship" (Exod. 31:3-5).

God equipped Bezaleel with special skills, and enabled him with special service to the Lord, and to teach others also. That is why when Moses conveyed the special plan to Bezaleel, God Himself unfolded the plan to Bezaleel, and changed the words of Moses into His Words, and through the gift of the word of wisdom, they were imprinted in the mind of Bezaleel. God also called Aholiab and other special assistants for the building of the Tabernacle.

It is that same wisdom which God has given to His children today who believe in Him. As children of God, we are God's Tabernacle (God's dwelling place). God has filled us with wisdom as we seek Him every day. I met a young lady some years ago who narrated a great testimony to me. She said that when she graduated from the university, she started searching for a job with her friends. She and her friends sent their applications to a particular company that needed workers with the type of skills that they studied in the university. The director of the company was willing to employ them, but on the condition that they will go to bed with him. The other girls agreed and got the job. This young lady was a born again Christian, and she held tenaciously to her God. The other girls put pressure on her to accept the offer and get the job, and take care of her life. This young lady vehemently refused. A few months later, a young journalist with a top job approached her, and they got married. The Lord blessed her with children. The husband was so wealthy that she did not need to work. She was extremely happy in her marriage, as she told me the story. Here we see a young sister filled with the wisdom of God. She stood with her head up, and depended on God, and He blessed her mightily. That is the same wisdom God has given to all of us today, to wait for the Lord for directions in this life. "Through wisdom is a house builded; and by understanding it is established" (Prov. 24:3). Children of God need divine wisdom to live in this world, with all its corrupt practices.

2. JOSHUA

Joshua, the son of Nun, was the successor to Moses. He was a general in the Israeli army, who conquered the Canaanites (Josh. 1:1; 24:31). Prior to the death of Moses, the Lord commissioned Moses to lay his hand on Joshua saying, "Take thee Joshua the son of Nun, a man in whom is the Spirit, and lay thine hand upon him" (Num. 27:18).

After the death of Moses, the Lord continued to assure Joshua concerning the land, and he continued to remind him to *"be strong and of good courage"* (Josh. 1:6-7). Joshua was physically strong as a great fighter, yet he was reminded of the Lord to "be strong and courageous." The Lord also reminded Joshua, "This book of the Law shall not depart out of thy mouth; but thou shall meditate therein day and night, that thou mayest observe to do according to all that is written therein: for then shall thou make thy way prosperous, and then thou shalt have good success" (Josh. 1:8).

Those who know and follow God's Word and law will be prosperous and successful, in that they possess the wisdom to live righteously and to achieve God's plan in their lives. The Word of God is wisdom itself which renders us strong and courageous in our everyday life.

Thus, Joshua gained wisdom when Moses laid his hand on him, and the Lord imparted wisdom. The Word of the law was also a source of wisdom for Joshua, as the Lord reminded him not to depart from it. It was through the wisdom of God, that Joshua was able to win great battles such as:

JORDAN

The first ever hurdle Joshua faced after taking charge over the nation of Israel, was to cross the Jordan River. The river was also overflowing at that time because it was the harvest season. However, the Lord instructed Joshua on what to do; "And the Lord said, And thou shalt command the priests that bear the ark of the covenant, saying, when ye are come to the brink of the water of Jordan, ye shall stand still in Jordan" (Josh. 3:8). When the priests that bare the ark dipped their feet in the brinks of the Jordan River, it swelled and rose on a heap, going a long distance from the city of Adam right to Zaretan (Jos. 3:15-16). This miracle took place according to the Word of the Lord. The whole nation of Israel revered Joshua. They all crossed the Jordan River on dry ground. When the nations across the Jordan heard what the Lord had done for the nation of Israel, and how they have crossed on dry ground over the River Jordan, the hearts of the people melted, and there was no spirit within them because of the children of Israel (Josh. 5:1).

JERICHO

The children of Israel were now faced with the first battle in the land that God had promised them. The city of Jericho was their first task they had to face. It was a huge city with iron chariots. The people were great farmers and very prosperous. When they heard that Israel had crossed the Jordan, the city gates were closed. Joshua was given specific instructions on the invasion of the city. "And ye shall compass the city, all ye men of war, and go round about the city once. Thus shall thou do six days. And seven priests shall bear before the ark seven trumpets of rams' horns: and the seventh day ye shall compass the city seven times, and the priests shall blow with the trumpets. And it shall come to pass, that when they make a long blast with the ram's horn, and when ye hear the sound of the trumpet, all the people shall shout with a great shout; and the wall of the city shall fall down flat, and the people shall ascend up every man straight before him" (Josh. 6:3-5). Joshua was relying on the wisdom of God, and not his own wisdom, as we find in the above verses, which led them to final victory when the city was captured, and the Canaanites were completely destroyed by the children of Israel.

The account of the battle of Jericho reminds me of a couple that were married for a few years, and were struggling to have children. They consulted a medical doctor, and nothing abnormal was discovered in the both of them. The pastor prayed about it, and the Lord directed him on what to tell the couple. The pastor asked them to fast for three days and three nights. When they completed the fast, a one-foot demon appeared and fought with them for three hours, and finally escaped out of the house. The following month, the woman became pregnant. Today, she is a mother of children and her testimony has encouraged others.

3. KING SOLOMON

King David was very old, and his son, Adonijah, took advantage to usurp power without his father, King David, knowing about it (1 Kings 1:5). This conspiracy was thwarted by Nathan the prophet, who told Bathsheba to present the case to the king. King David swore to Bathsheba and promised that Solomon will be king after him (1 King 1:29-30).

When Solomon was anointed king over Israel, he first made sure that all his enemies were eliminated, in order to consolidate his kingdom (1 Kings 1:23-46). Solomon loved the Lord to the extent that the Lord appeared to him in a dream, and asked him:

"Ask what I shall give thee" (1 Kings 3:5).

King Solomon replied and told the Lord;

"Give me now wisdom and knowledge, that I may go out and come in before this people; for who can judge this thy people, that is so great? And God said to Solomon, because this was in thine heart, and thou hast not asked riches, wealth, or honour, nor the life of thine enemies, neither yet hast asked long life; but hast asked wisdom and knowledge for thyself, that thou mayest judge my people, over whom I have made thee king: Wisdom and knowledge is granted unto thee; and I will give thee riches, and wealth, and honour, such as none of the kings have had that have been before thee, neither shall there any after thee have the like." (2 Chron. 1:10-12).

The Lord granted King Solomon wisdom, knowledge, riches, wealth and honor, to the extent that none of the kings before and after him ever had. King Solomon became the wisest king on earth. It was King Solomon who wrote most of the book of Proverbs, Song of Solomon, and Ecclesiastes. King Solomon's wisdom became apparent when two harlots appeared before him, asking for his wise counsel. Both of these women had children. Unfortunately, one of the women slept on her child, and the child died. She exchanged the child while the other woman was sleeping (1 Kings 3:19-21).

In the ensuing argument between the two women trying to claim the living child, King Solomon asked for a sword to divide the living child, and to share him between the two of them. One of the women cried out when her bowels could not withstand such an act. She said to the king;

"Oh my Lord, give her the living child, and in no wise slay it" (1 Kings 3:26).

The other woman cared less, and asked for the child to be slain. It was then that King Solomon intervened and said; "Give her the living child, and in no wise slay it: she is the mother thereof. And all Israel heard of the judgement which the king had judged; and they feared the king: for they saw that the wisdom of God was in him, to do judgement" (1 Kings 3:27-28). It is through the wisdom of God, that King Solomon could build a magnificent temple in Jerusalem. This turned out to be one of his greatest achievements, which also turned out to be the center of worship throughout Israel. During the inauguration of the temple, King Solomon prayed and called upon Yahweh to bless His people, and to hear their prayers when they present themselves in the temple (1 Kings 8:22-54). Solomon's reputation spread to distant lands, even as far as Sheba in Arabia. He was visited by the queen of Sheba, who wanted to see Solomon's glory and riches, and to also see the depth of his wisdom. Solomon's reputation was heard in distant lands, as God had blessed him with wisdom and riches.

The failure of Solomon came in when he started drifting from God. He was married to strange wives, in which God had forbidden the children of Israel to do. He became arrogant, and did not listen to the wise counsel of the elders, which led to his undoing. As children of God, we should always hold on to God's wisdom.

4. DANIEL

Daniel was a captured Jew from the nation of Israel. When king Nebuchadnezzar of Babylon invaded the land of Israel, he brought in a lot of slaves to Babylon. Daniel became a servant in the king's palace, where he found favor with the prince of the eunuchs. While he was in the palace of the king, he became a chosen vessel used by God to liberate thousands of his people. God also bestowed on Daniel great wisdom in several circumstances (Dan. 1:17; 5:11; 6:3).

Due to the great wisdom that Daniel possessed in interpreting dreams, which the wise men in Babylon could not interpret, the king fell down prostrate before Daniel, and worshiped his God. The king admitted that the God of Daniel was the *"King of kings"* with all the power and glory. Daniel was promoted to the highest position in the kingdom. The king gave Daniel gifts, and made him ruler over all the province of Babylon. He was also made chief of the governors over the wise men of Babylon because of the wisdom he obtained from God. His three friends, Shadrack, Meshach, and Abed-nego, were in control of the affairs over the provinces of Babylon (Dan. 2:48:49).

Despite the blessings in Babylon, Daniel and his friends never compromised their faith. They stood their ground, even when they were thrown in the furnace and in a den of lions. Can any of us live like Daniel? When we are obedient to God, His wisdom will manifest in our lives.

HOW TO RECEIVE THE WISDOM OF GOD

1. THROUGH THE WORD OF GOD

The Lord said to Joshua; "This book of the law shall not depart out of thy mouth; but thou shalt meditate therein day and night, that thou mayest observe to do according to all that is written therein: for then shalt thou make thy way prosperous, and then shalt thou have good success" (Josh. 1:8). Joshua was asked by the Lord to be faithful to His Word, by talking about it, (cf. Deut. 6:7), and meditating on it day and night (cf. Psalms 1:2). To mediate means to read quietly or to talk to yourself, as you think about what you have read, and how it applies to your life. To make your way prosperous and have good success means that those who know and follow God's Word, will be full of wisdom, and prosper in the Lord, as they live a righteous life, and also strive to attain God's goal in their lives. God's Word is supposed to be an authoritative guide in our lives, as believers in Christ who study God's Word daily. Christ Himself said; "Search the Scriptures; for in them ye think ye have eternal life: and they are they which testify of me" (John 5:39).

When we study the Word of God and meditate over it, we are imparting the wisdom of God in our lives. Prophet Isaiah also had this to say: "And the Spirit of the Lord shall rest upon him, the spirit of wisdom and understanding, the spirit of counsel and might; the spirit of knowledge and of the fear of the Lord;" (Isaiah 11:2).

When Jesus came to His own country and taught in the Synagogue, His countrymen marveled at his wisdom, and said; "Where did this man get this wisdom and these mighty works?" (Matt. 13:54). The words that Jesus spoke came from the Father. He never spoke with His own authority. As children of God, we are to depend on God because He is the source of our wisdom, knowledge, and power.

The Lord Jesus Christ said in Matthew 7:24: "Therefore whosoever heareth these sayings of mine, and doeth them, I will liken him unto a wise man, which built his house upon a rock." Children of God are not only to read the Word of God and meditate over it, they are also to apply it in their everyday life. This will bring transformation of life in the individual.

2. DEVELOPING THE RIGHT RELATIONSHIPS

Amos 3:3 says;"Can two walk together, except they be agreed?" As children of God, the type of people we associate with will influence the life we live. The apostle Paul had this to say; "Be not deceived: evil communications corrupt good manners" (1 Cor. 15:33).

There is a popular saying that says, "show me your friends and I will tell you who you are". This saying is true because the type of friends you have, will determine the type of conversation you will get yourself into, or the type of outward behavior that you will portray to the world. "He that walketh with wise men shall be wise: but a companion of fools shall be destroyed" (Prov. 13:20). The people you associate with will affect your character. If you associate yourself with other children of God, you will behave like them. The types of conversations they involve themselves in when you are with them, will influence the way you speak to others, and will also affect your thinking. "Perverse disputings of men of corrupt minds, and destitute of the truth, supposing that gain is godliness: from such withdraw thyself" (1 Tim. 6:5). We are not to associate with people with *"corrupt minds"*. They will affect our behavior. We are to depend on the Holy Spirit for directions.

3. BY LAYING ON OF HANDS BY A MAN OF GOD

The apostle Paul wrote to Timothy saying; "Wherefore I put thee in remembrance that thou stir up the gift of God, which is in thee by the putting on of my hands" (2 Tim. 1:6).

Timothy was supposed to stir the fire that was imparted into him, by the laying on of hands by the apostle Paul. The gift of God in us must be fueled, as we depend on the Holy Spirit through prayer and fasting. Joshua, the son of Nun, was full of the spirit of wisdom, when Moses laid his hands on him (Deut. 34:9). Believers should note that we are to grow daily, and know God deeper, as we are in this spiritual journey here on earth.

THE BENEFITS OF WISDOM

1. WISDOM MAKES YOUR ENEMIES HELPLESS

I will present below some passages from the Bible to strengthen your faith: "For I will give you a mouth and wisdom, which all your adversaries shall not be able to gainsay nor resist" (Luke 21:15). There is a function of the Holy Spirit, in the life of the believer that will direct him on what to say in front of his enemies. "When a man's ways please the Lord, He maketh even his enemies to be at peace with him" (Prov. 16:7). Your enemies know that you are a child of God, and there is nothing they can do, but to make peace.

"For wisdom is a defence, and money is a defence: but the excellency of knowledge is this, that wisdom giveth life to them that have it" (Eccl. 7:12). Wisdom is greater than money. It will also protect you from the ills of this life, just as money does also, but the fact is that money can disappear in thin air, but wisdom will never disappear. It will always remain with us. "For the Lord giveth wisdom: out of his mouth cometh knowledge and understanding (Prov. 2:6). God will always give us what He has promised, if we do what he has taught us in His Word. To deliver thee from the way of the evil man, from the man that speaketh froward things (Prov. 2:12). The only way a believer can be delivered from this evil world, is to depend on the wisdom and knowledge of God. To deliver thee from the strange woman, even from the stranger which flattereth with her words" (Prov. 2:16). It is through the wisdom and knowledge of God that a believer can be delivered from the spirit of lust and immorality.

2. WISDOM CREATES FAVOR AND RECOGNITION TOWARD YOU

"Exalt her, and she shall promote thee: she shall bring thee to honour, when thou dost embrace her" (Prov. 4:8). "Blessed is the man that heareth me, watching daily at my gates, waiting at the posts of my doors. For whoso findeth me findeth life, and shall obtain favour of the Lord" (Prov. 8:34-35). "My son, forget not my law; but let thine heart keep my commandments: So shalt thou find favour and good understanding in the sight of God and man" (Prov. 3:1, 4).

3. WISDOM GUARANTEES PROMOTION

"By me kings reign, and princes decree justice. By me princes rule, and nobles, even all the judges of the earth" (Prov. 8:15, 16). The Holy Spirit has the authority to direct a believer on how to take wise decisions that will please his people, just as King Solomon did in the beginning of his reign in Israel.

"And thou Ezra, after the wisdom of thy God, that is in thine hand, set magistrates and judges, which may judge all the people that are beyond the river, all such as know the laws of thy God; and teach ye them that know them not" (Ezra 7:25). God gave Ezra wisdom on how to select magistrates and judges, who will know how to rule God's people through wise council.

"Exalt her, and she shall promote thee: she shall bring thee to honour, when thou dost embrace her. She shall give to thine head an ornament of grace: a crown of glory shall she deliver to thee" (Prov. 4:8-9). As children of God, we are to make our decisions based on the wisdom of God (Bible). In every decision we make as believers, God should receive the glory. It is shameful that among believers in the church, we sometimes want things to go our own way, rather than putting God first.

4. WISDOM GIVES LIFE AND HEALTH

"My son, attend to my words; incline thine ear unto my sayings. Let them not depart from thine eyes; keep them in the midst of thine heart. For they are life to those that find them, and health to all their flesh" (Prov. 4:20-22). "Be not wise in thine own eyes: fear the Lord, and depart from evil. It shall be health to thy navel, and marrow to the bones" (Prov. 3:7-8). The Word of God is the wisdom of God, and we are advised to read it and study it daily. It is through the study of the Bible, that we are going to understand the abundant life and health that God has given to us as believers.

THE LEADING OF THE HOLY SPIRIT

One of greatest challenges that Christians face today, is the leading of the Holy Spirit. It is when we are constantly close to God that the Spirit (the will of God) can take control over the soul (personal desires). Once we call ourselves children of God, we have to battle every day to abide by God's Word and to adhere to His directions. The greatest tragedy that many Christians face is that they are taught about the Holy Spirit, but they do not accept His leadership. Some Christians even think that the leading of the Holy Spirit is only occasional; no, it is not. It is the source of our new life and the source of our strength. It is through the leading of the Holy Spirit that we can walk closely with God. However, we should note that the Holy Spirit cannot be operational in an individual without first looking at the Cross. The Cross simply means that we are dependent on God. It is when we depend on God that the Holy Spirit becomes operational in the life of a Christian. The Holy Spirit and the Cross are dependent on each other. One cannot do without the other. The Holy Spirit becomes highly operational because it is always looking at the Cross. The Holy Spirit makes room for our inner man to grow to the extent that we start becoming spirit beings.

As believers in Christ, we all know something concerning the operations in the Spirit, but we have not yet understood the laws which govern its functioning. As children of God, we are to learn how to develop our intuitions to the extent that there will be no outside interference. The challenges we Christians face is the uncertainty about our intuitions. Many do not know the normal state of their spirit where they could lean on. This does not mean that they do not receive revelations from God, but they always fall short of understanding how they can be led by the spirit. For believers to be consistently led by the Spirit, they must understand the laws that govern them, and the will of God in their lives. To develop our spirit, we should do the following:

1. We are to search the Word of God because it is the source of our wisdom. (John 5:39).
2. We are to fast and pray (Luke 4:12-13; Isaiah 58:6).
3. We are to meditate on the Word of God (Josh. 1:8)
4. We are to fellowship with other children of God (Acts 4).
5. Our thought life also plays a very important role because it is from there that we can know whether what we have received comes from our soul or from our spirit.

This can be done when we are reflecting on something. In such situations, we should think where the source of our thoughts comes from; if it is our feelings, we should think from which direction it is coming from. It is imperative that we distinguish our soul from our spirit. This is extremely important in our walk with the Lord.

Our soul helps us to examine things from our own perspective, which is dangerous to us because pride can easily creep in. The soulish life revolves around our own "self-pride or self-pity", as Watchman Nee puts it. Children of God *"must apprehend the true condition of their inward parts through the knowledge accorded to them by the Holy Spirit".* The believer has to be conscious of the fact that the Spirit of God is in him or her. While the soul is affected from outside influences, the Spirit is influenced from the inside. The Spirit is always independent of the soul, and it is not affected by the conditions around the person. The danger a believer faces is that he can be confused between the soul and the Spirit.

A soulish Christian will lean towards reason or emotions and in some cases, he may fall into the trap of thinking that the thoughts from their soul is that of the spirit because of their former thought life. It is when they are experienced in the things of the Lord that they can know the difference between the soul and the spirit. We may be able to discern our intuitions in such occasions. As children of God, we should also learn how to weigh outside influence and our spirit being. People may tell us stories out of their experiences, but the spirit may be opposed to their ideas (1 Cor. 14:29). We should learn to receive from our own spirit, and not from man. If our spirit agrees, then it is good; if not, reject it. This ability should be with those who are already experienced with the things of the spirit. If they are still learning, they should yield to more experienced people around them and follow their counseling. Even the apostle Paul made it clear that the gospel he preaches, was not revealed to him by man, but by God Himself.

If we are preachers, we should learn to receive from God, what we are to preach. It is from there that we can start learning from God's wisdom. It is not just receiving from instructors, or preaching what other people have preached or taught. Below this chapter, we are going to discuss, in some detail, how people have been led by the Spirit in different ways, such as in dreams, visions, angels, revelations, etc., in the New Testament. The apostle Paul wrote in the book of first Corinthians: "But as it is written, Eye hath not seen, nor ear heard, neither have entered into the heart of man, the things which God hath prepared for them that love him. But God hath revealed them unto us by his Spirit: for the Spirit searcheth all things, yea, the deep things of God" (1 Cor. 2:9-11).

In the previous chapter, we learned that as children of God, our wisdom comes from God, and not from the world and its system. As we begin to grow in Christ, it becomes more and more apparent that we are to depend on the wisdom of God because without it, we will not discover God's revelation, and where it is leading us in our daily walk with Christ. Prophet Isaiah had this to say; "For since the beginning of the world men have not heard, nor perceived by the ear, neither hath the eye seen, O God, beside thee, what he hath prepared for him that waiteth for him" (Isa. 64:4).

As believers, God has prepared mighty things which can only be discovered as we abide by Him. These are not things that depend on human intelligence or in the physical realm of life. They are revealed to us in the Spirit. If the Scriptures are revealed to us through divine revelation, God also has in store for us many things He wants to reveal to us.

I will want us to look very closely at the phrase in verse 10, *"the deep things of God"*. If there are deep things which God wants to reveal to us, then there are *the shallow things* which will be revealed to those who have not totally surrendered to God. Verse 10 is one of the greatest statements ever made by Paul in his epistles. We see this in our daily walk with God.

I remember when I used to work in Cameroon as a research linguist and literacy consultant with many of my colleagues from the western world. Some of us from Africa will tell our European friends what the Lord had revealed to us, and what we are supposed to do as directed by the Lord. Those of us from Africa were not taken seriously until what we told our western colleagues began to take place exactly as it was revealed to us by the Lord. Some of our European colleagues were stunned and they confessed to us that there is something that they from the west have to learn from us Africans. We African believers not only study the Word, but we also fast and pray seriously to find out where the Lord is leading us. We want to discover the spirit realm and also get deeper into the mind of God.

When the Lord Jesus Christ was about to leave the world, He told His disciples; "But the Comforter, which is the Holy Ghost, whom the Father will send in my name, he shall teach you all things, and bring all things to your remembrance, whatsoever I have said unto you" (John 14:26).

Yes, the Holy Ghost is prepared to teach believers all that they ought to know about all things. All that we ought to know comes from the Word of God, and through fasting, prayers, meditation, and fellowship with other children of God. It is when we do these things, that we will have deeper revelations from God. The earthly ministry of our Lord Jesus Christ started with fasting and prayers (Matt. 4:2; Luke 4:2). The ministry of the apostle Paul started after he had fasted for three days and three nights (Acts 9:9).

When the Lord called me in 1983, I was very excited, and I started going to church and attending Bible study. A few weeks later, I decided to fast as I studied from Scriptures. That night after the fasting, the Lord revealed to me that He has called me to fight a battle. From that time, I decided to fast once a week. Later on, I started fasting more than a day a week. I realized that I was getting deeper revelations from God. As I decided to discipline myself before the Lord, He started revealing to me deep spiritual things that were taking place in my family, in the church, and about my own friends. I will like us to discuss some godly people in the Bible, and how they were led by the Spirit in the New Testament. This will allow us to learn from them.

THE ANGEL APPEARS TO MARY

The angel appeared to a woman called Mary, and said to her;"Fear not, Mary: for thou hast found favour with God. And, behold, thou shalt conceive in thy womb, and bring forth a son, and shalt call his name JESUS" (Luke 1:30-31). From these two verses, we find that God uses people who find favor with Him. Mary was a virgin, and she was honest with her God. God does not care about our status in society. One would have thought that God will appear to the daughters of kings, Pharisees, Sadducees, or notable people in the society. NO! God is looking for just and humble people who acknowledge Christ as their Savior. The way of life we live can influence God to use us for His glory.

MARY VISITS ELISABETH

The angel of the Lord also appeared to Zacharias the priest, and promised him that his wife, Elizabeth, will deliver a son. When Elizabeth was pregnant, she was visited by Mary (Luke 1:39-40). When Mary entered the house of Elizabeth and greeted her, the baby leaped in her womb, and Mary said, "And blessed is she that believed: for there shall be a performance of those things which were told her from the Lord" (Luke 1:45).

From this passage, we see that when believers meet together, the Lord may reveal something which may reinforce what we already know. Mary went further to say, "My soul doth magnify the Lord, And my spirit hath rejoiced in God my Saviour. For he hath regarded the low estate of his handmaiden: for, behold, from henceforth all generations shall call me blessed" (Luke 1:46-48).

The soul here refers to the mind and thoughts of Mary. She was extremely excited. The spirit here is what relates to God. Mary was excited, and her spirit was moved within her.

As believers, there are moments when our mind is uplifted. We are excited about something, and we start to praise the Lord with our spirit.

THE AGED-SIMEON

According to the Jewish culture, every male child was supposed to be circumcised on the eighth day. "As it is written in the law of the Lord, every male child that openeth the womb shall be called holy to the Lord: And to offer a sacrifice according to that which is said in the law of the Lord, A pair of turtle doves, or two young pigeons" (Luke 2:23-24).

Baby Jesus was brought to Jerusalem to fulfill the days of purification according to the Mosaic Law. It happened that Simeon, who was a devout man and full of the Holy Ghost, had a revelation through the Holy Ghost, that he will not see death before he has seen the Lord Jesus Christ (Luke 2:26). When the child Jesus was placed in his arms, he could DISCERN through the power of the Holy Ghost, that this was the Son of God, the Savior of the world-*"a light to lighten the Gentiles and the glory of.... Israel"* (Luke 2:32).

I will want us to look at some personal qualities of Simeon. In Luke 2:25-27, there are four qualities which mark Simeon as a pious and godly man:

1. He was a just man.
2. He was a devout man.
3. He was a Spirit-filled controlled man.
4. He was living in anticipation of the Lord's coming.

As children of God, we need these qualities of Simeon, to be led by the Spirit. The revelation Simeon had about the coming

Savior, was through the Holy Ghost. When he saw the child Jesus, he could discern immediately. As children of God, there are certain revelations that come only through the Spirit of discernment (1 Cor. 12:10). There are many of us who have this gift, and we need to use it for the kingdom of God.

The question we should ask ourselves is, "how do we know the voice of the Lord, and how do we receive it"? In 1 Corinthians 2:12-13, we read:

"Now we have received, not the spirit of the world, but the Spirit which is of God: that we might know the things that are freely given to us of God. Which things which also we speak, not in the words which man's wisdom teacheth, but which the Holy Ghost teacheth; comparing spiritual things with spiritual."

What the apostle Paul is saying here is that through the inspiration of the Holy Ghost, the writers of the Bible were inspired to write the Word of God (2 Tim. 3:16; 2 Pet.1:20). Those of us today who have received Christ, are also inspired to receive messages from God. Through the inspiration of the Holy Spirit and from the Word of God, we are able to know what we ought to know from God.

When God wants to speak to His children, He speaks in a quiet voice, which is followed with an administration in our inner mind. Jesus said in John 10:5 and 14,

"And a stranger will they not follow, but will flee from him: for they know not the voice of strangers."

"I am the good Shepherd, and know my sheep, and I am known of mine."

When the voice of the Lord is speaking to us, we will definitely know, as the Lord Jesus Christ has said in the above passage. We are to obey immediately because the Spirit of the Lord searches all things. We are not to grieve the Holy Spirit through disobedience (Eph. 4:30). We are not to quench the Holy Spirit when God is delivering us a message. We are to lay a foundation whereby God can build upon. Our dependency should be on Christ alone.

As children of God, we should cultivate the habit of waiting on God, especially when speaking in tongues. Sometimes, after speaking in tongues for a long time, God may want to drop something in your spirit. You will feel it impressing into your spirit. In such moments, be quiet for a moment, receive it and pray about it immediately. God may be leading you to arrest a situation in the spirit. Sometimes, after you have finished praying for a long time, do not just get up immediately. Be quiet before the Lord for a while. A message from His throne may change your life forever!

There are also moments when the Spirit of God is impressing on you to go and pray. Obey it, because God may be calling you to intervene in a situation. I remember a story when a brother was directed by the Holy Spirit to pray. He immediately went on his knees, and started praying in the Spirit, because the Lord did not tell him what exactly to pray for. He was carried in the Spirit, and prayed for eight hours. When the burden was over, he stopped praying. The Lord told him in a quiet voice, "My son, the devil wanted to take your daughter's life, but your prayers have saved her". It happened that this brother had traveled, and the daughter fell sick. She was in the operating room with the doctors, fighting for her life. Through obedience and prayers, the daughter's life was saved.

THE FLIGHT INTO EGYPT

The wise men from the East came to Jerusalem to search for the child, Jesus, in order to worship Him. When they met Herod the king, he directed them and told them that when they find the child, they should come back and tell him, so that he can also go and worship the child (Matt. 2:8). As the wise men were directed by the

this aside, and did what the angel of the Lord told him. There is a big lesson for us to learn here. When God tells us to do something, or if God reveals something to us in a dream, we should not delay. We should act on it immediately because nobody knows what will happen if we delay. Joseph acted immediately because it was to him that the revelation was given. It was not given to the leader of the church. He did not need to seek advice from anybody. Joseph did not question God about why he should flee to Egypt with the wife and child, even knowing that the child was very tender, and that the mother did not need such a tedious journey, just after delivering Jesus. Joseph did not question God about why he should escape by night, even knowing the dangers of the desert, where there are scorpions, snakes, and coupled with the hazardous environment. The night is a dangerous time. It is a time when the crime rate is high. They may be attacked by thieves or a wild animal. All these, Joseph brushed aside, and yielded to the angel's warning.

As children of God, do we yield to what God is directing us, or do we seek council from others, so that they could reason us properly? I know of a sister in the Lord who ran away from her husband's house. When the pastor heard the news, he invited this sister, and persuaded her to go back to her husband's house. The sister told the pastor that she knew the husband too well. She said that if she goes back, the husband will kill her. The pastor persuaded her, and told her that such a thing will never happen. He escorted the woman to the husband's house, and tried to settle their differences. That particular night, the husband slaughtered the wife. If this woman had stood her ground, she would have been alive today. I am not rejecting the fact that we should seek counsel from leaders of the church, but when God reveals something to you, act as you have been told. You know your problem more than anyone else.

Let us imagine that Joseph did not obey the message from the angel of the Lord. What do we think could have happened to Jesus?

We are told in the Scriptures that when the wise men did not return to Herod, he was very angry, and he slew all the children that were in Bethlehem, who were two years and below. Can we imagine the tragedy that would have taken place if Joseph had disobeyed? We thank God that Joseph's action was a fulfillment of Scriptures, which was spoken by Jeremiah the prophet, "Thus saith the Lord; A voice was heard in Ramah, lamentation, and bitter weeping; Rachel weeping for her children refused to be comforted for her children, because they were not" (Jer. 31:15).

As Christians, God may be leading us to do something that we never thought of. God may be calling us to carry out a task that may change the lives of other people, or even an entire nation. Before the Armenians were slaughtered by the Ottoman Turks, a young Christian fasted for seven days and seven nights, eating no food or drinking any water. Breaking the fast on the eighth day, God opened his eyes in a vision, and he drew a map as directed by the Holy Spirit. The Lord told him that all the Armenians should move to the West coast of the United States. Many heeded and left, while others did not believe and remained. When the Ottoman Turks invaded the land, they slaughtered all the Armenians that remained. Yes, disobedience is as the spirit of witchcraft!

When Herod was dead, an angel of the Lord appeared to Joseph again in a dream saying, "Arise, and take the young child and his mother, and go into the land of Israel: for they are dead which sought the young child's life. And he arose, and took the young child and his mother, and came into the land of Israel" (Matt. 2:20, 21).

Joseph, through a dream, again obeyed the Lord, and brought the young child to Israel by night, as it is fulfilled in the Scriptures; "Out of Egypt have I called my Son" (Matt. 2:15).

When they arrived in Israel, Joseph was directed again in a dream to dwell in Nazareth, which was the fulfillment of the Scriptures;

"He shall be called a Nazarene" (Matt. 2:23).

Throughout the entire story, Joseph was directed by the Lord. He responded promptly, and did what God wanted him to do with the young child. As children of God, we should learn to depend on God, and not on man. The church and its leaders are to help us grow closer to God, but they cannot take the place of God in your life. God has anointed us as kings and priests here on earth. Children of God have a kingdom to rule. God has established a government, and we are to obey that constitution handed to us, which is the Bible.

THE OUTPOURING OF THE HOLY SPIRIT

Prior to the death and resurrection of Jesus Christ, the Lord had prayed for His disciples (John 17). He had promised the Comforter (John 14: 26), and after His death and resurrection, "being assembled together with them, commanded them that they should not depart from Jerusalem, but wait for the promise of the Father, which, saith he, ye have heard of me. For John truly baptized with water; but ye shall be baptized with the Holy Ghost not many days hence" (Acts 1:4, 5).

The Lord Jesus Christ promised them again saying; "But ye shall receive power, after that the Holy Ghost is come upon you: and ye shall be witnesses unto me both in Jerusalem, and in all Judaea, and in Samaria, and unto the uttermost part of the earth" (Acts 1:8).

When Jesus finished speaking, He was taken into heaven. Here, we find something interesting. Jesus gave His disciples specific instructions. Did they follow it? Yes, they did. When God gives us specific instructions, just as Joseph and the wise men, do we follow them? Do we become frustrated because it is taking too long for it to manifest? The disciples followed the instructions of the Lord. They all returned from the Mount of Olives to Jerusalem. What did they do next? "These all continued with one accord in prayer and supplication, with the women, and Mary the mother of Jesus, and with his brethren" (Acts 1:14).

As we read further, Judas the traitor, was replaced by Matthias, after prayers and casting their lots. They were all in one place waiting for the promise until Pentecost. "And there appeared unto them cloven tongues like as of fire, and it sat upon each of them. And they were all filled with the Holy Ghost, and began to speak with other tongues, as the Spirit gave them utterance" (Acts 2:3-4).

Their obedience to the Lord Jesus Christ yielded what was promised. Many of us today lose the promise of God or delay his promises because of our impatience. How long does something take for you to wait patiently for it? Do not take short-cuts!

At Pentecost, Jews from all nations gathered together under heaven, and they were all amazed to hear their languages spoken by the apostles. At Pentecost, Peter was emboldened. This was the promise of the Father in Joel 2:28-32. It was proclaimed by John the Baptist, and it was referred to many times by our Lord Jesus Christ Himself (John 7:37-39; 14:16-17; 15:26; 16:6-7, 13-14; Acts 1:8).

The power of the Holy Ghost manifested in Peter, and he could now address his people boldly. Let us not forget that this was the same Peter who denied Christ thrice (Matt. 26:34, 74; Luke 22:61). He was timid in the beginning. He had to repent thrice for him to be restored. At Pentecost, the power came from heaven to Peter and to the other apostles. Peter's message was short and straight to the point; it was simple, plain and clear; it was also instructive and informative; and it was not based on emotional evangelism. His message came from Scriptures, and could be proven from Jewish history. He was also bold, fearless, and unapologetic. In Acts 4:13, the people looking at Peter and the other apostles, saw them in three ways:

1. The miracles they performed in the name of our Lord Jesus Christ.
2. They spoke with boldness before their accusers (verses 18-21).
3. Despite the fact that Peter and John were forbidden by the leaders from preaching the gospel (verses 8-10, 12), their behavior was characterized as holy tenacity, as they proclaimed the gospel.

The apostles were prepared to stand in the name of Our Lord Jesus Christ, and face persecution. Their tenacity to see Jesus proclaimed, led to great results (verse 4).

PREACHING THE GOSPEL TO OTHER NATIONS

Since the resurrection of our Lord Jesus Christ (Acts 1:9), and the consequent outpouring of the Holy Spirit (Acts 2:3-4), the gospel was only preached in Jerusalem, in contrary to what we have been told in Acts 1:8 that the gospel will be preached to the uttermost parts of the earth. The persecution that started in Jerusalem, was a means of forcing the disciples to come out of their comfort zone, and go to other distant lands to preach the gospel.

Sometimes, God may want us to leave our comfort area, and go to other areas where we never thought of. We may be having our own plans, while God is having a different plan in our life. The persecution in Jerusalem led to the death of Stephen (Acts 7), and later, on the emergence of Saul who consented on the death of

Stephen. Saul later received letters from the chief priest, and headed for Damascus, where he could arrest other Christians, and throw them in jail. Little did Saul know, that the hunter will become the hunted. As he approached Damascus, a light shined upon him, and he fell down. A voice spoke to him: "Saul, Saul, why persecutest thou me?"

Saul asked, "Who art thou Lord? And the Lord said, I am Jesus whom thou persecutest: it is hard for thee to kick against the pricks" (Acts 9:4, 5). The Lord instructed Saul to go to Damascus where the Lord also instructed Ananias to go and pray for Saul, who was fasting and because he was blind. When Ananias prayed for Saul, his eyes were opened immediately. This was a shock to Saul. The first thing he did was to withdraw to Arabia to find out about this new doctrine (Gal. 1:15-17): "But when it pleased God, who separated me from my mother's womb, and called me by his grace, To reveal his Son in me, that I might preach among the heathen; immediately I conferred not with flesh and blood: Neither went I up to Jerusalem to them which were apostles before me; but I went into Arabia, and returned again unto Damascus."

Saul had been brought up by Gamaliel in Jerusalem to be a Pharisee. He knew that he was a godly man. His withdrawal to Arabia gave him the opportunity for the Lord to reveal to him Jesus in the Old Testament. As soon as Saul, who later became Paul, got this revelation from God, that was when he went back to Damascus, and declared, to the amazement of all, that Jesus Christ is Lord.

Saul, who later became Paul, is revealing to us something very important. In Arabia, he now had a perfect understanding of the will of God in his life. He knew that the Lord has sent him to preach the gospel to the Gentiles. That was his calling. He knew it, and that was his mission. When he came to Jerusalem, the apostles were afraid of him, and did not believe that he had been called by the Lord. It was Barnabas who took the bold step of bringing him among the apostles (Act 9:26, 27). In Jerusalem, Paul started preaching the gospel with boldness, declaring that Jesus Christ is Lord.

It is very important for us Christians to know what God has called us for in His vineyard. Unfortunately, many Christians are satisfied just staying in the church, and listening to the preacher, without knowing exactly what their true calling is. If we do not know true our calling, it will be difficult for us to properly identify the talents that God has blessed us with. There are some lessons we can learn from Saul's conversion:

1. His conversion was unexpected, since nobody can believe that God would convert him. If the Christians of Saul's day were asked whether God will convert Saul, they would have sworn that God will never do such a thing to a man, who was full of such an evil heart. Saul was a Pharisee and bigoted fellow, who was an enemy of the church. However, let us not forget, that it is God that does the conversion, and not man. It is the same thing today. We see certain people, and we doubt whether God will ever convert such people. In Christ, there is nothing impossible.
2. Saul was suddenly and dramatically converted. The dramatic intervention of the Lord is seen in Acts 9:22 and 26, when he was on a journey to Damascus to imprison the Christians. After being struck on the way by the Lord Jesus Christ, this proud and rebellious fellow, now becomes a penitent and humble fellow before Christ. He was saved in a flash of lightning. It was a total turnaround from his former position. This is a real and genuine conversion. This is like passing from death to life. Look at John 3:3 and John 5:24. With most people, the Holy Spirit makes a gradual impression upon the heart, the conscience, and the mind,

until we totally surrender to the Lord Jesus Christ. Has this process been going on in your life? If it is true, then your conversion can be sudden; for at this moment, you can be saved.

3. Saul actually saw the Lord, and heard His voice. Every believer has seen the Lord through faith. We see Him on the Cross dying for us (Isaiah 53:5); we see Him rising again in our lives (1 Corinthians 15:4); we see Him ascending (Acts 1:9-10); we see Him exalted at the right hand of the Father (Heb. 1:3); and we hear His voice in His Word. But Saul was struck down by the Lord, and he heard His voice talking to him. This dramatic conversion was not a sunstroke, epilepsy or a delusion; if it had been any of these, his life would not have been transformed as we see in 2 Corinthians 5:17.

Saul's conversion was not like others, in the sense that:

a. The sovereignty of God began it. It was God who did it, and not man; and no human being would have prevented it. It was a supernatural work of grace, a miracle.
b. It was altogether of grace and not of works. Saul's conversion had nothing to do with his previous life. He did not bring any offering that was acceptable to the Lord. All he did was to accept salvation from the Lord (Eph. 2:8-10, Titus 3:5).
c. Saul had a personal encounter with the Lord. Saul's interview was personal and private, as we learn from Acts 9:4-6. It was a total shock to him because he believed that Jesus Christ was an impostor, and was dead and buried; and that he never rose again. However, in a flash of lightning, he realizes that Jesus is alive and well, and He is the Son of the Most High God. He is the true Messiah and in-bearer;

> He is sitting on the right hand of the Father; and He is the Lord and Savior of all. This revelation takes place in every conversion.

When Saul saw the Lord on his way to Damascus, he was full of guilt for the following reasons:

a. He knew he was a sinner and needed a Savior (1 Tim. 1:15)
b. He knew that Jesus alone could save him (Acts 9:5 cf. Matt. 1:21).
c. He was overwhelmed with the Lord's compassion (Acts 9:5).
d. He totally yielded to our Lord Jesus Christ (Acts 9:6-22).

PHILIP IN SAMARIA

As the apostles started dispersing from Jerusalem, Philip moved to Samaria to preach the gospel. The people of Samaria believed the gospel Philip preached, seeing the miracles which he did (Acts 8:7). "For unclean spirits crying with loud voice, came out of many that were possessed with them: and many taken with palsies, and that were lame, were healed." Philip baptized the people of Samaria, and when the news went to Jerusalem, Peter came also to Samaria, and joined Philip. They baptized the people of Samaria in the name of the Lord Jesus Christ. They laid their hands on the Christians, and they were baptized in the Holy Ghost.

However, there was a man in Samaria named Simon, who had gained great popularity among the people. He bewitched the people of Samaria with his sorcery, and was seen as a great man. Let us pause here awhile, and look at this closely, because in many churches, Christians are looking for miracles, and not Christian character. Especially in Pentecostal churches, when we hear that a man of God is in town, instead of us going to listen to the message of the Lord, what we are interested in is seeing a miracle. Do we really take the time to find out who these people are? Do we pray and allow the Holy Spirit to lead us? The people of Samaria did not, and as a result, they were bewitched, and became blind witches hiding in the Synagogue. How many blind witches are there in our churches today, and they do not even know it? Thanks be to God that He will always deliver His children out of their ignorance, just as we read that Philip did in Samaria.

When the people of Samaria believed, Simon the sorcerer also believed. When he saw the people of Samaria receive the baptism of the Holy Ghost, he thought he could use money to buy that power. Peter rebuked Simon the sorcerer, and said: "Thy money perish with thee, because thou hast thought that the gift of God may be purchased with money. Thou hast neither part nor lot in this matter: for thy heart is not right in the sight of God. Repent therefore of this thy wickedness, and pray God, if perhaps the thought of thine heart may be forgiven thee. For I perceive that thou art in the gall of bitterness, and in the bond of iniquity" (Acts 8:20-23).

Peter was not prepared to compromise the ministry of our Lord Jesus Christ. He saw the sin of Simon, and he did not want to partake in such an act. He rebuked him openly. I begin to wonder how many men of God have corrupted themselves with money. They receive money from people, and they do not know their original intent, which might actually affect their ministry in the long run. Christians need to be sensitive in the spirit, and not allow themselves to be influenced by people. There are many church leaders who have corrupted other leaders, and they were seen as people who are dedicated to the Lord. They were given positions in the church, only to discover that some of them were the synagogue of Satan hiding in the house of God.

A lesson to learn from Simon the sorcerer, is that people mistakenly took him to be a great man of God. They saw the miracles he was performing among them, and they were carried away with his sorcery. The number of that people were demonized in Samaria is something that we do not know. The point I am trying to raise is that we should learn to ask God certain things before we make a decision. We live in a time where people are carried away by miracles, without knowing who that "miracle worker" really is. Simon the sorcerer was exposed when the Holy Ghost came to Samaria. I wonder how many agents of darkness have been exposed in our churches today. Many church services have become ritualistic, and the power of God has been swept under the carpet. Many churches appear as if Jesus is asleep, and many congregants are content with it. The church of Jesus Christ needs to be alive in the Spirit, and should manifest the power of God. A typical example is the church that started in Jerusalem. Let us look closely at what happened, and compare with our churches today.

In Acts 2:41-47, we have a pattern for the whole dispensation of what the church should be like. If we want to know how our local church looks like, compare it as it is found here in the passage of Scripture. The foundation of the church was not laid by man, but by Christ. In Matthew 16:18, we find the promise of our Lord Jesus Christ, and it is exactly what we find in Acts 2:41,47. It was Jesus alone who added those in the church who were saved. For a church to be created, we have to preach the gospel, and the Holy Spirit will convict the people, the miracle of the new birth will take place, and those who are born again are added to the Lord. Today, I will ask the question as a challenge to all of us; how many of our members have received the miracle of the new birth, and how many of them can testify what Jesus has done in their lives?

The church was openly committed to Christ. The gospel was preached to them by Peter, and they were convicted of their sin, and had repented and received the Word, as seen in Acts 2:37-40. Those who received the Word, were baptized. What a baptismal service to find 3000 people baptized in a service! Can we have that today?

Another point is that they were all united in Spirit. All who trusted Christ as their personal Savior, were together. In Galatians 3:28, we see how this togetherness looks like. They grew together, for "they continued steadfastly" (Act 2: 42). They all fed upon the Word of God because they were all fellowshipping together. They all remembered the death of Jesus Christ together during the breaking of bread. They all prayed together, shared together whatever they had (verse 44), and rejoiced together (V. 47).

PHILIP AND THE ETHIOPIAN EUNUCH

After Samaria, the angel of the Lord spoke to Philip saying: "Arise and go toward the south unto the way that goeth down from Jerusalem unto Gaza, which is desert. And he arose and went: and, behold, a man of Ethiopia, an eunuch of great authority under Candace queen of the Ethiopians, who had the charge of all her treasure, and had come to Jerusalem for to worship, was returning, and sitting in his chariot read Esaias the prophet. Then the Spirit of the Lord said unto Philip, Go near, and join thyself to this chariot" (Acts 8:26-29).

In the above passage, Philip obeyed as directed by the angel. It was prompt and without delay. God was leading Philip to meet a man who needed some help. Philip went not knowing what he will meet on his way. As a coincidence, he met an Ethiopian eunuch. Notice that Philip was led by the Spirit. How many of us have been led by the Spirit, yet we want to first seek the counsel of man before obeying the Lord? This is the greatest challenge we face in the church today. Philip did not ask Peter before going toward Gaza. He just went as directed by the angel of the Lord. The Ethiopian eunuch was reading a portion of Scripture that he did not understand. God used Philip to change this man's life forever. He explained the passage to him, and the man asked Philip to baptize him. After the baptism, Philip was carried in the Spirit to Azotus, where he continued preaching the gospel until he arrived at Caesarea.

Why God sent Philip to preach and baptize an individual, and then be carried away in the Spirit, can only be explained by God alone. It may be that God was preparing the Ethiopian eunuch to preach the gospel, or to do something else when he goes back. Only God can tell. However, there is something we can learn from this encounter. The Ethiopian eunuch was now properly converted. He now had a proper understanding of what he was reading. It is a day he will never forget. No Christian on earth can forget the day he was converted. There is always a testimony to give. It is a day you find yourself moving from darkness into life. The man from Ethiopia was well educated and probably very wealthy, since he was in charge of the queen's treasury. He was no ignoramus, as some people will accuse some Christians to be. From Africa, he was reading the scroll of Isaiah the prophet. The passage he read permeated his Spirit, and he just needed somebody to open his spiritual eyes. There are many things that the queen's treasurer will remember.

a. The queen's treasurer will never forget where he was converted. Born again Christians will never forget what happened during their conversion. They will always remember where, when, and how they were converted. The pertinent thief was converted on the cross. Zacchaeus and Matthew the tax collector will never forget the day of their conversion. Do you remember the day you were converted?
b. The queen's treasurer will never forget the person who converted him. The Word of God is quick and powerful, as the Hebrew writer says. We can be hardened as a rock, but the Word of God will always do its work. Philip was

used by the Lord in the life of this man who was yearning to know God.

c. The queen's treasurer will never forget the portion of Scripture that converted him. He will never forget Isaiah 53, especially verses 5 and 6. I remember the first day I went to church. The preacher preached on the parable of the prodigal Son (Luke 15:11-32).
d. The treasurer will never forget his baptism by Philip, as written in Matthew 28:19-20. He will not forget the joy he had when he was converted.

As the work of God is great and the laborers are few, we may not be carried away in the Spirit like Philip. However, some of us do find ourselves in our dreams; preaching in distant lands; praying for people; or even carrying out a crusade. We may think that it is an ordinary dream. It is not! As children of God, God is using our Spirits to carry out His work for His glory.

In Nigeria, some Muslims in the north have come to the south, and confessed to the Christians that a man called Jesus has appeared to them in their dreams, and has warned them to receive Him as their personal Savior or face the consequences. These are testimonies that are true, and nobody can explain what is really happening. The Christians in the southern part of Nigeria and Cameroon have been fasting for the Muslims in the northern part of the country, and God is listening to their prayers.

PETER IN LYDDA AND JOPPA

The apostle Peter had left Samaria, where he preached the gospel with Philip. He was traveling to other areas, and finally arrived at Lydda, where he healed Aeneas, who was bed-ridden for eight years. God used Peter to raise this man from his bed, and all the people turned to the Lord (Acts 9:34-35). Our churches need this power today as never before. People want to see before they believe. Believers have this power today, and God wants to use us for his glory here on earth. God wants to use us to close the mouth of sceptics, and turn them to the Lord.

From Lydda, Peter now came to Joppa, where he met Tabitha, which by interpretation is called Dorcas. Dorcas was known in her community for the good works she did and her alms-deeds (Acts 9:36). When she died, two men were sent to Lydda, to bring Peter to Joppa, to intercede for her. When Peter arrived, he prayed for her, and she woke up (Acts 9:40). The power of God through Peter, led to all the people of Joppa to believe in the Lord Jesus Christ.

CORNELIUS THE CENTURION

Peter finally came to Joppa, where he was lodging with Simon a tanner. While in the house, he decided to go and pray in the housetop, where he found himself in a trance, where all sorts of four-footed animals appeared to him, and a voice told him to rise and eat. This occurred to him thrice, and he refused to eat because, from birth, he has not eaten anything thing that was common or unclean (Acts 10:9-16). The appearance of these four-footed beasts was meant to prepare the mind of Peter. He was originally called to preach the gospel to the Jews, and not to the Gentiles. Now we find a situation whereby God was preparing him to meet Cornelius, who was a Gentile. What a surprise! Have we found ourselves in situations where the Holy Spirit is leading us to do something we never thought of? This may happen to any child of God.

While Peter was contemplating on this vision, two men were sent by Cornelius to go to Joppa to a specific house at the sea side, and they will meet a man called Simon surnamed Peter (Acts 10:17-18). In this episode, we find God in action. God can answer our prayers in a variety of ways. An angel just spoke to Cornelius, directing him what to do, and he obeyed.

The men who were sent, were at the gate waiting for Simon Peter, and the spirit of the Lord spoke to Peter to follow them immediately (Acts 10:12). God may direct us sometimes to do certain things which may not be in our agenda. However, when the Holy Spirit speaks, we are obliged to obey immediately, just like Peter.

The story of Cornelius is a record of the conversion of a Roman soldier, who was a Gentile. As a centurion, he had one hundred soldiers under his command. Despite the fact that Cornelius was a soldier, he became a saint. Cornelius is the first Gentile to be admitted into the Christian faith. The account of Cornelius tells us that he was religious, God-fearing, prayed regularly, and payed alms (Acts 10:1-3).

When Peter arrived in the house of Cornelius, he reminded them and said, "Ye know how that it is an unlawful thing for a man that is a Jew to keep company, or come unto one of another nation, but God hath shewed me that I should not call any man common or unclean (Acts 10:28).

Here we learn certain things:

1. The salvation of a sinner is the sovereign work of the Almighty God. We are told that Cornelius was seeking for God, but I am very sure that it was God who was seeking for Cornelius. In Acts 8 specifically 8:29, it is the Holy Spirit that is prominent. In Acts 9, it is the Lord Jesus who is prominent (Acts 9:4-6). In Acts 10:3-6, we find out that it is God who is prominent. Our salvation is planned by the Lord; the Son procures our salvation; and it is the Holy Spirit that perfects our salvation in our hearts and in our lives.

2. The Lord has many ways of reaching or bringing a soul to Himself. When we compare Acts 8, 9, and 10, we find that God does things in mysterious ways. God approaches people in different ways, such as the Queen's Treasurer, Saul of Tarsus, and then to Cornelius.
3. God is no respecter of persons. Nobody, as regards to race, position in society, education, or social standing, has a better chance than anyone else of being saved. This is made clear through the vision given to Peter (Acts 10:9-16, 28). Compare this to Romans 3:29-30 and Romans 10:12-14.
4. A good man needs salvation just as much as a bad man. In Acts 10:2, it is apparent that Cornelius was a good man, but he needed salvation, just as any bad man like Saul. Jesus came to seek and to save that which was lost. We are all sinners, and we need salvation through our Lord Jesus Christ. We can compare Isaiah 64:6; Romans 3:23; James 2:10; and Romans 3:20.
5. The only condition of salvation, is faith in Our Lord Jesus Christ. In Acts 10:2, Cornelius was a good man that paid alms, but he needed to be saved, just as much as the worst soldier under his command. People find it difficult to understand that no matter how good you are, you still need salvation through Our Lord Jesus Christ. In Luke 18:9-14, Jesus compared a Pharisee and a Publican. The Publican, who felt that he was a sinner, went home more justified than the Pharisee, who thought he was righteous. We are all sinners before God, and we need salvation (Acts 10:44-45). When we compare Isaiah 64:6, Romans 3:23, James 2:10, and Romans 3:20, we find that we are all sinners.
6. The gift of the Holy Spirit is the evidence of salvation. This is made clear in Acts 10:44-45. Salvation is an inward experience called born again (John 3:3). Salvation is the

impartation of a new life (2 Pet. 1:4), and it is brought through the impartation of the Holy Spirit.

7. Baptism is a command of the Gospel. Peter had no option but to baptize them (Acts 10:47). With their new found faith, they urged Peter to stay with them for a few days (Acts 10:48).

THE MACEDONIAN CALL

The apostle Paul was on his second missionary journey, and was revisiting the churches in Asia, in order to consolidate them (Acts 16:4-5). The work of consolidation is as important as the work of evangelizing the unconverted. This is what Christians should always reflect on. It is very good to convert people, but it is more important for them to bring them to a position, whereby they serve the Lord more effectively. As Paul went on preaching, he wanted to spread the gospel to other areas in Asia. In Acts 16:6-7, the Holy Spirit intervened and forbade Paul to preach the gospel in Asia. It is important to note that it is the Holy Spirit that directs us or constrains us sometimes, by opening a door or sometimes by closing it, as we carry out His work. Paul humbled himself and obeyed the new direction of the Lord. It is through this obedience, that the gospel was preached in Europe for the first time (Acts 16:9).

In the night, Paul saw a vision. A man in an unevangelized continent at the time was beckoning him to come. It is very important for us to pause for a while, and note all of the nine visions that have direct bearing on the spread of the gospel in the book of Acts-Acts 7:55; 9:5; 9:10; 10:3; 10:11; 16:9; 18:9; 22:17: and 23:11. Does the Lord still constrain us in the preaching of the gospel? The answer is yes! My first call into the ministry was directed by the Lord, to preach the gospel in the prison ministry. That was where

I started; where God molded me spiritually, and then opened the door to other areas.

As mentioned earlier, in the night, Paul saw a vision, and that vision was directed to him and nobody else (Acts 16:9). "And a vision appeared to Paul in the night; There stood a man of Macedonia, and prayed him, saying, Come over into Macedonia, and help us."

There are many Christians today whom God is calling to help in preaching the gospel. Millions of souls for whom Christ died for, do actually cry out now, in words that are full of pathos and urgency, "Help.... Help.... Help!". These are people of different tongues and races all over the world. The appeal is not only to help, but to go and preach the gospel to the people who cry out for the gospel. It is a cry to all doctors, nurses, agriculturalists, teachers, carpenters, builders, etc. It is not just for pastors to preach the gospel alone. It is an appeal for men and women of all walks of life, who will live and preach the gospel where there is a need. Where do you fit into the picture? In which area can you help?

Paul knew that this was an opportunity, given to him by Jesus Christ. He would not delay. He obeyed immediately. When we look at the characteristics of his obedience in verse 10, we see that it was prompt obedience; it was bold obedience, and it was pin-pointed obedience.

The victories he experienced were,

1. A number of people were converted, such as Lydia (verses 14 and 15), and the jailor (verses 24-34).
2. The grace of Jesus Christ was strikingly manifested. It was costly for Paul and Silas, as verses 19-24 show us, but what a victory they gained! Their backs were bleeding, and their feet were in the stocks, yet look at verse 25. Here is grace in action; grace that is sufficient in time of need, and in every situation.

BARNABAS AND SAUL

After the conversion of Saul, the apostles were still afraid of him, when he tried to join them. However, Barnabas took the courage, and brought him to the other apostles, and testified how Saul had seen the Lord on the way; and how he had spoken to him; and how he had preached the Word boldly in Damascus. Saul now had the opportunity to preach the Word in Jerusalem because of the intervention of Barnabas (Acts 9:26-29).

As the gospel was spreading to other nations, Barnabas was sent to Antioch to preach the gospel. He exhorted the Christians in Antioch to remain in the Lord. However, he had no peace in him. He had seen Saul, who later became Paul, preach in Jerusalem. He was convinced that he should go to Tarsus, the birthplace of Paul, and bring him to Antioch (Acts 11:25-26). There are certain qualities we find here in the life of Barnabas:

1. He was a man of faith (verse 24).
2. He could discern the work that was before him in Antioch, and felt that he needed a co-worker with other gifts to complement the work of God (verse 26).
3. Barnabas was a humble man. He was not selfish to think that things must go the way he wants. His interest was to see the advancement of the kingdom of God (verse 26).
4. He was a man who wanted to help others in times of necessity. When Agabus prophesied in Jerusalem that there will be scarcity in Jerusalem, he decided to send relief from the Christians in Antioch to those in Jerusalem. The new disciples all contributed according to their ability (Acts 11:28-30).

While at Antioch, there were certain prophets and teachers in the church. These were the ways in which they lived their life in the church:

1. They ministered the Word of God to the church (Acts 13:2).
2. They lived a life of fasting and prayers in the church at Antioch (Acts 13:2-3).
3. They obeyed the direction of the Lord; for the Holy Spirit directed them to set apart Barnabas and Saul for the ministry (Acts 13:2). Let us pause here for a minute, and reflect on what the Lord is doing here. How many Christians will obey the direction of the Holy Spirit, when they realize that the work of God is not going the way they thought, or they become satisfied with what they have, and want to remain in the same spot? Barnabas and Saul did not question the direction of the Lord. The next thing they did was to fast, pray, and ask for the grace of God to be with them. We should note that despite the great number of converts in Antioch, Paul and Saul still had to leave. Certainly, God Himself will raise other people among the disciples to continue the work left behind by Saul and Barnabas.
4. Barnabas and Saul wasted no time. They immediately left for their new assignment that the Lord had called them for. They did not sit down to question how the Christians in Antioch will be fed spiritually.
5. They saw it as an opportunity to preach the gospel in other places.

When they came to Paphos, they met a Jewish sorcerer and false prophet, whose name was Bar-jesus (whose name by interpretation is Elymas the sorcerer), that tried to persuade the deputy to turn away from the faith. "Then Saul, (who is also called Paul,) filled with the Holy Ghost, set his eyes on him, And said, O full of all subtilty and all mischief, thou child of the devil, thou enemy of all righteousness, wilt thou not cease to pervert the right ways of the Lord? And now, behold, the hand of the Lord is upon thee, and thou shalt be blind not seeing the sun for a season. And immediately there fell on him a mist and a darkness; and he went about seeking some to lead him by the hand" (Acts 13:9-11).

Here we observe certain things:

1. The kingdom of God must advance, despite the challenges we face in the field.
2. Paul acted promptly to show the power of God to his hearers.
3. The deputy, after seeing the power of God, was converted immediately. The kingdom of God must be advanced through violence.
4. It taught a lesson to the people in Paphos, to know that the power of God is more powerful than the power of Satan. In Acts 8, which we earlier studied, Simon, who was another sorcerer, that thought he could buy the kingdom of God with money, was also silenced by Simon Peter. Elymas faced instant judgement, and became blind for a season. What a great victory for the kingdom of God. God is looking for great men today, who will exert the power of God on earth, so that those hardened unbelievers will know that there is a God, who is the same yesterday, today, and forevermore (Heb. 13:8).

I remember when I and a friend were called to preach the gospel in a certain village. The Lord directed us to fast and pray. We fasted for seven days before going to the village. Upon arrival, there was a crusade scheduled for that evening. We were directed to preach in a hall, which was used by members of an occult society. The fire of the Lord came down that evening, and miracles took place. Many people believed, and they came out and gave their lives to Christ. On the third day after the crusade, a young girl came and confessed that she was a witch. She had been polluting crusades with the spirit of fornication, telling lies, engaging in hatred and division among Christians, and doing other things that would not help the church to grow. She said that the power of God has arrested her, and she had to confess it. When she was asked where her power was, she said that she was hiding it in her armpit. My friend laid her hands in her armpit, and commanded it to go to the eternal lake of fire. That young lady was delivered, and she is now serving the Lord faithfully.

LYDIA OF THYATIRA

The conversion of Lydia is found in two verses of Acts 16:14-15. "And a certain woman named Lydia, a seller of purple, of the city of Thyatira, which worshipped God, heard us: whose heart the Lord opened, that she attended unto the things which were spoken of Paul. And when she was baptized, and her household, she besought us, saying, if ye have judged me to be faithful to the Lord, come into my house, and abide there. And she constrained us." The apostle Paul had an opportunity to preach the gospel to some God-fearing women. At the riverside in Philippi, these women, of whom one of them was Lydia of Thyatira, met regularly for prayers. She was an obscure humble woman, who contributed through her open heart, for the gospel to be passed on to Europe. This is a case where God will use ordinary people for His glory. When God wanted to enter a continent where many people would be saved, He chose Lydia of Thyatira.

Lydia attended prayer meetings. She was sincere in her serving the Lord, but she was not born again (John 3:3). She had not been saved through faith in Jesus Christ (John 5:24). Her heart had not been opened to welcome the Savior Jesus Christ (John 1:11-12).

How many people are in our churches today, who serve the Lord faithfully, but are not born again? One thing that makes a person a Christian, is the presence of the Lord Jesus Christ in their heart and in their life (Rev. 3:20). It is not enough to believe in God; we must believe and trust in the Lord Jesus Christ as well (John 14:1).

Lydia heard the message that was preached, and it saved her. As she listened, faith became operative in her heart. This is the way God works. He is sovereign in the salvation of our soul, and when we are told that Lydia "attended" the words that Paul spoke, it means that she payed attention to the full presentation of the gospel by Paul. She heard him declare the truth of John 3:16; Acts 4:12; and Romans 1:16. She heard about the person and work of Christ, and as she heard, her heart opened, and the Lord Jesus Christ came in.

Immediately as the Lord entered her heart, she was baptized with all the members of her household. So here again, we have the Scripture order: (1) believe on the Lord Jesus Christ and be baptized; (2) receive Him as the Savior, (3) and confess Him openly as Lord (Matt. 28:18-20; Acts 2:41). This is God's ordained method of confessing that Christ is our Savior. Her public baptism must have been a testimony to others.

Lydia and her entire household were baptized, which means that everybody in the house believed on the Lord Jesus Christ as their personal Savior. In Psalms 68:6 we read that "God setteth the solitary in families".

What does that mean? Lydia is an example of this statement. God saved Lydia, and through her, the members of her household came to know the Lord.

Just as faith without works is dead, the works of Lydia were shown publicly. Opening her home to other men of God, was proof of her open heart. This could be compared to Zacchaeus' restitution, as evidence of his conversion (Luke 19:8).

THE DAMSEL

In acts 16:16-18, we find another strange situation. Saul and Barnabas went to pray when a damsel with the spirit of divination, who brought a lot of money to her masters, met them and cried out saying; "These men are the servants of the most high God, which shew unto us the way of salvation. And this did she many days. But Paul, being grieved, turned and said to the spirit, I command thee in the name of Jesus Christ to come out of her. And he came out the same hour." (Acts 16:17-18). As Christians, we want to abide closely to the Lord, and at the same time, we want to listen to the voice of the Lord, and receive directions from Him. We know that once you have received Christ, you are no longer yourself; you are now owned by Christ. As a child of God, you must always listen to the Lord. The challenge and question we must ask ourselves is, "Do we take time to ask the Lord where we are going? We move from one crusade to the other. We want to see the power of God. We want to also see miracles taking place, or we want to know what God has to tell us personally. This is good. There is nothing wrong about it, but have we asked the Lord whether we should attend that crusade in the first place, or who really is that man of God, and of what spirit he is using? Paul was preaching the way of salvation; he was preaching Christ, and wanted the people to believe in Him, who was pierced on Mount Calvary for our sins.

At the other end of the scale, we find another young lady, who was a fortune teller. She told the people the truth, just like she was telling the people about Paul and his followers: *"These men are the followers of the Most High God who have come to shew us the way of salvation."* This was true, but of what spirit was she using? We have seen the case of Simon the sorcerer, who was healing people, and they saw him as a great man of God, when, in actuality, he was really bewitching the people with his sorcery (Acts 8). We get carried away by the crowd, without taking a step backwards and asking ourselves, "Who is this man or woman"? As children of God, we need to be alert and alive in the Spirit. We always need to ask God before we make a major decision concerning our lives. Many of us have suffered from the spirit of error because we do not ask the Lord for direction, or for the Lord to give us the greenlight before we move.

In the passage concerning Paul and the damsel, the apostle Paul could discern that, though the damsel was speaking the truth, she was using a different spirit. Paul wasted no time in rebuking the spirit, which left her the same hour. As children of God, we should not waste time in putting the devil where he belongs, and that is under our feet. When Paul came to Paphos, as we saw earlier, he met an obstructionist to the gospel, Bar-jesus, who was known as Elymas the sorcerer. He wasted no time in commanding him to be blind for a season (Acts 13:11).

Children of God, let us not forget the promise of the Holy Spirit in Acts 1: 8: "But ye shall receive power, after that the Holy Ghost is come upon you: and ye shall be witnesses unto me both in Jerusalem, and in Judaea, and in Samaria, and unto the uttermost part of the earth." Yes, Christ has given us enormous power to put the devil where he belongs. The devil should not be a hindrance to our ministry, because we have been given that authority.

I remember a young man of God who fasted for forty days. At the end of his fasting, he was invited by a young girl in the church, to come and break his fasting in her house. He prayed and left for the girl's house. When he arrived at the young lady's house, she prepared food for him, and placed it on the table. As the young man was blessing the food, he was carried in the spirit, and prayed in tongues for almost an hour. This young girl started transforming, and became an old woman. The young girl later confessed that she was a witch, and wanted to destroy the young man. God is looking for men and women that He can use to destroy the works of the devil, just as the apostles did.

What can we learn from this? This damsel was foretelling the truth. However, this is the danger that many Christians fall into. We may find people who foretell the truth to us, but we never find out who they really are, and what spirit they are using. They may be mighty spiritual healers, just like Simon the sorcerer, but under what spirit?

Sometimes, we find ourselves in places, where our spirit is uncomfortable with the people around us. The Lord is giving us a signal that we should either leave or adjust our relationship.

Through the power of the Holy Ghost, God can use us to carry out deliverance in certain environments, in order to push back the kingdom of darkness. The deliverance of this damsel must have caused chaos in the society because the masters lost their source of revenue, but this brought glory to the kingdom of God. The book of Mark 16:17-18 gives us these great promises: "And these signs shall follow them that believe; In my name shall they cast out devils; they shall speak with new tongues; They shall take up serpents; and if they drink any deadly thing, it shall not hurt them; they shall lay hands on the sick, and they shall recover."

God also protects His children from accidental harm made by their enemies. These signs are only for them that believe, and these signs were conferred to others who worked extraordinary miracles. "They shall take up serpents and it shall not hurt them", can be seen in the life of Paul when a serpent fastened on his hand, and nothing happened to him (Acts 28:3-6). This is a great promise to believers,that the old serpent who deceived Eve, is unable to do any harm to those of us who believe. If children of God are compelled to drink any poison, God is able to protect them from the hands of their enemies. This does not mean that when we see poison, we should drink it. This is tantamount to tempting God.

LESSONS LEARNED

Our study on the leading of the Holy Spirit, has some particular lessons for us all. Anyone who engages in the service of the Lord, must be filled with the Spirit. In Acts 4:31, we notice that when the apostles prayed, the whole place was filled with the Holy Spirit, and they preached the Word of God with boldness. In Acts 5:3, the presence of the Holy Spirit in the life of Peter, exposed the duplicity of Ananias and his wife Sapphira. How glorious it is when children of God are filled with the Spirit! The lessons we have learned are as follows:

1. *When God is truly working, the devil will also be at work.*

In Acts 5:17-18, we learn that the apostles were under severe persecution. Behind that persecution is Satan himself at work. God was doing a mighty work in the lives of the apostles, but Satan was also well awake, and at work also. This teaches us that the more we want to fast, pray, and preach the gospel, the more Satan is also determined to thwart the work of God. Those Christians who are lukewarm should understand that they are on the devil's side. When we give ourselves to prayers and the Word of God, we will overcome Satan.

2. *It is always safe to trust God when we are doing His will.*

In Acts 5:18-19, we learn that despite the fact that the apostles were jailed, they were released by the angel of the Lord. Many people are in prison in different parts of the world because they are Christians. God is still visiting them and carrying out miracles in their lives. God broke the prison doors, and let loose the apostles. When we are in "prison", we should trust the Lord for His deliverance.

It is the same thing when our faith is tried. We are to trust God for a miracle in our lives. This brings more glory to God, and blessings to our lives.

3. *We ought to obey God rather than man.*

"Then Peter and the other apostles answered and said, we ought to obey God rather than man" (Acts 5:29).

This shows boldness and great courage in the life of the apostles, to say this to the Jewish leaders. Despite the threats, Peter and the other apostles were determined to preach the gospel. What a great commission the Lord Jesus Christ handed to them (Matt. 28:19-20). That same commission is handed to us today.

4. *God gives the Holy Spirit to those that obey Him.*

This principle is enunciated in Acts 5:32. "And we are his witnesses of these things; and so is also the Holy Ghost, whom God hath given to them that obey him" This means that when we repent and believe on the Lord Jesus Christ, God will give us the Holy Ghost. It also means that when we completely surrender our lives to the Lord Jesus Christ, He fills us and empowers us. The measure that God will fill us and empower us with, depends on our level of obedience.

5. *To be effective in doing the work of God, we must acknowledge the importance of the Holy Ghost.*

Peter made this fact in verse 32. This is a great fact about the book of Acts. A witness is someone who shows forth Christ, and talks about Christ. A witness is a demonstration of Christ, a sample of the grace of God, and a living illustration of what God can do with a man or a woman. We are to surrender all that we are and have to the Lord, and we must receive all that the Lord offers to us, in the person and power of the Holy Spirit.

6. *When God initiates a work, He will prosper and complete it: it cannot be overthrown.*

We find this in verses 38-39. Gamaliel told his audience: "And now I say unto you, refrain from these men, and let them alone: for if this counsel or this work be of men, it will come to nought: But if it is of God, ye cannot overthrow it; lest haply ye be found even to fight against God." This should give all of us courage in times of difficulties; that we have a God who will always lead us to a victorious end.

THE SECRET POWER THROUGH PRAYER

The church is striving and searching for ways in which it can grow, but on the contrary, God is looking for people that He can use to overthrow the kingdom of darkness here on earth. This can be done through prayer. When churches use earthly methods to promote God's work here on earth, they forget that "The eyes of the Lord run to and fro throughout the whole earth, to shew himself strong in the behalf of them whose heart is perfect toward him" (2 Chron. 16:9). God is looking for people whom He can use to exert His power here on earth through them. God needs men and women of prayer whom the Holy Spirit can direct to do mighty things. Prayer is the key that opens the door, and makes the impossible, possible .For the church to be successful, it needs better men that God can use. "There was a man sent from God, whose name was John" (John 1:6). It was John who prepared the way for the Lord's coming. God needs people whom He can use to prepare the way for His second coming. How many people today know that? We spend a lot of time in reading other books and making great sermons, but forget one cardinal point that keeps the church of God flowing with power; and that is prayer.

Sometimes, we get ourselves involved in how to get the church to grow, and forget the perfect example in Acts of the Apostles. In

Acts 6:4, we learn that as the ministry was expanding, the apostles gave themselves to prayer and to the Word. Church administration was given to other leaders of the church, who were elected by members of the congregation, and were full of the Holy Ghost.

Every member of a congregation has a high calling, and must not ignore it. For you to discern your calling just as Paul did, you should be a man or woman of prayer. We receive great revelations through prayer. Every man or woman who calls himself or herself a servant of God, must be a prayer warrior. For you to be a prayer warrior does not mean looking for a time when you have to pray; being a prayer warrior means that you give your total self to it. It is a serious work in which you dedicate yourself to it.

I remember when I was ordained as an elder in a church of about a thousand people. I asked the Lord, "Lord, I want You to tell me who these people are that you have directed me to take care of". I spent all night praying for thirty days, and what the Lord opened my spiritual eyes to see were really mind-bothering. From the leaders to many members of the congregation, there were many people who were agents of darkness. I asked myself, "How did these people get to these positions?" The Lord said to me, "It is because the pastors never prayed to get approval from Me." I was full of rage in the spirit, and I started praying them out of the church. Some left when the Holy Spirit exposed them. Some went into a spiritual fight, but at the end, they backed down through the power of prayer. One thing I never did was accuse anybody of being an agent of darkness. All I did was to pray, and let God do His work.

WHY PEOPLE SHOULD PRAY

People generally like to talk about prayer, but how many people really practice it? Prayer is the greatest weapon against Satan and his demons; yet, many people neglect prayer, or sometimes, we are so much in a rush that we just murmur and go away. If we want to learn more about prayer, we should go to the Bible itself. There is a lot to learn about prayer. People of prayer are focused, and they know what they are praying for. They are not in a rush. They are interested in getting results for the time that they have spent before God. When the apostles gathered together, they prayed, and the place was shaken; and they were all filled with the Holy Ghost, and spoke the Word of God with boldness (Acts 4:31).

A good example of learning about prayer is from our Lord Jesus Christ. "And it came to pass in those days, that he went out into a mountain to pray, and continued all night in prayer to God. And when it was day, he called unto him his disciples: and of them he chose twelve, whom also he called apostles" (Luke 6:12-13). Here, we learn a good example from our Lord Jesus Christ. He spent an enormous time talking to the Father prior to making such a bold step before His ministry started. He knew that the decision He will take will affect His entire ministry throughout His stay here on earth, and also when He departs to be with the Father in heaven.

Before we make any major decision, such as choosing a partner in marriage, do we really spend time in prayer to find out what God has for us, or where the Holy Spirit is directing us? It is a tragedy that most people look at the outward appearance, rather than being led by the Holy Spirit. God may be leading us to something which we do not like in the present moment, but the God who knows the future, knows what is good for us.

Thus, there are many reasons why we should pray:

1. *The Lord commanded us to pray.*

"And he spake a parable unto them to this end, that men ought always to pray, and not to faint" (Luke 18:1). We are obliged to pray and seek the Lord's face in prayer every day. The apostle Paul told the church in Thessalonica that they should, "Pray without ceasing" (1 Thess. 5:17).

2. *Prayer is the key to spiritual breakthrough.*

At the time when persecution of Christians was taking place in the nation of Israel, Herod killed James, the brother of John, and when he saw that it pleased the people, Simon Peter was also imprisoned. Fortunately, the whole church gave itself to prayer without ceasing, and finally, the Lord intervened by sending an angel to deliver Simon Peter, as we see below. "And, behold, the angel of the Lord came upon him, and a light shined in the prison: and he smote Peter on the side, and raised him up, saying, Arise up quickly. And his chains fell off from his hands. And the angel said unto him, Gird thyself, and bind on thy sandals. And so he did. And he saith unto him, Cast thy garment about thee, and follow me" (Acts 12:7-8).

3. *God enjoys our companionship when we seek Him in prayers. He enjoys our communion with Him.*

"And there will I meet with thee, and I will commune with thee from above the mercy seat, from between the two cherubims which are upon the ark of the testimony, of all things which I will give thee in commandment unto the children of Israel" (Exod. 25:22).

4. *Prayer brings "inner peace and inner satisfaction".*

When you spend a lot of time in prayers, you will find your external circumstances changing. God will touch the heart of people around you, and miracles will start taking place.

5. *Prayer brings an inner pleasure in your life.*

Mike Murdock said, when you pray, your spirit is fed the essential "bread of life". Prayer is as necessary for your spirit, as food is for your body. "Come unto me, all ye that labour and are heavy laden, and I will give you rest" (Matt. 11:28).

6. *Prayer brings blessings to others.*

The light of God will shine around you and the people in your family.

When believers bring the problems of others before God, and when all their needs are met, that brings satisfaction and blessings to you.

"And the Lord turned the captivity of Job, when he prayed for his friends: also the Lord gave Job twice as much as he had before" (Job 42:10).

"I exhort therefore, that, first of all, supplications, prayers, intercessions, and giving of thanks, be made for all men" (1 Tim. 2:1).

7. *Prayer is a great and mighty door for God to show us His power and miracles in our present generation.*

"Call unto me, and I will answer thee, and shew thee great and mighty things, which thou knowest not" (Jer. 33:3).

8. *Through prayer, you can change the destiny and future of your life.*

"If my people, which are called by my name, shall humble themselves, and pray, and seek my face, and turn from their wicked ways; then will I hear from heaven, and will forgive their sin, and will heal their land" (2 Chron. 7:14).

9. *The importance of prayer is to resist the devil and his evil schemes.*

"For we wrestle not against flesh and blood, but against principalities, against powers, against the rulers of the darkness of this world, against spiritual wickedness in high places. Wherefore take unto you the whole armour of God, that ye may be able to withstand in the evil day, and having done all, to stand" (Eph. 6:12-13).

10. *Prayer leads to spiritual power and spiritual growth which brings blessings into the family and into the church.*

"Search me, O God, and know my heart: try me, and know my thoughts: And see if there be any wicked way in me, and lead me in the way everlasting" (Psalms 139:23-24).

"Ask, and it shall be given you; seek, and ye shall find; knock, and it shall be opened unto you. For every one that asketh receiveth; and he that seeketh findeth; and to him that knocketh it shall be opened" (Matt. 7:7-8).

11. *Prayer is a powerful and mysterious weapon that man cannot fully understand.*

Our duty as humans is just to pray and wait on God for an answer. If we pray, things happen. Does this mean that if we do not pray, things will not happen? The answer to this question is that God does not answer a prayer without a means. He is sovereign, and that is why our prayers are important. Prayer is the means in which God accomplishes His will. The more we pray, the more things happen, especially when we pray according to His will. When we are called to pray, we should understand that it is a great responsibility placed upon our shoulders. A powerless Christian is one that doesn't take time in prayers. "The effectual fervent prayer of a righteous man availeth much" (James 5:16b). "Ye lust, and have not: ye kill, and desire to have, and cannot obtain: ye fight and war, yet ye have not, because ye ask not. Ye ask, and receive not, because ye ask amiss, that ye may consume it upon your lust" (James 4:2-3).

12. *Prayer brings wisdom.*

The Word of God is very explicit about this. "If any of you lack wisdom, let him ask of God, that giveth to all men liberally, and upbraideth not; and it shall be given him" (James 1:5).

13. *Prayer can tame an unruly tongue.*

Christians, who have learned the fullness of prayer, have learned to control the tongue. They have learned the truth of James 3:8. "But the tongue can no man tame; it is an unruly evil, full of deadly poison."

"Set a watch, O lord, before my mouth; keep the door of my lips" (Psalms 141:3).

14. *Prayer brings revival in a church.*

It can settle church disputes and misunderstandings among believers. Prayers can root out heresy, and bring revival in the church.

15. *Prayer brings salvation.*

When we intercede for others, God will intervene and change their lives. I know of a brother who prayed for five years, for his junior brother to be converted.

16. *Prayer strengthens a minister, and brings wisdom and power into the pulpit.*

THE POWER OF PRAYER

1. *The greatest weapon any Christian has here on earth is prayer.*

It is a means in which we can communicate to God. It is through prayer that we unleash the supernatural power of God. In Psalms 62:11, the Bible says, "God hath spoken once; twice have I heard this; that power belongeth unto God."

2. *It is through prayer that we can expand the Kingdom of God here on earth.*

"Power belongeth unto God", and it is through our asking that we can receive that power.

3. *The first apostles and Christians were men of prayer.*

Their prayer life led to the manifestation of God's power in their lives. Many Christians were added because they saw the power of God (Acts 2:46-47).

4. *The apostles revealed the source of their power when they told the congregation:*

"But we will give ourselves continually to prayer, and to the ministry of the word" (Acts 6:4). Because they gave themselves to prayer, there was that abounding love, the power of God, and fruitfulness of the Spirit of God, among them (Acts 2:44-47).

5. *The power of prayer cleanses us from known and unknown sin.*

"Who can understand his errors? Cleanse thou me from secret faults. Keep back thy servant also from presumptuous sins; let them not have dominion over me: then shall I be upright, and shall be innocent from the great transgression" (Psalms 19:12-13).

6. *Prayer brings a true sense of knowledge of ourselves.*

Through prayer, we can easily identify our strengths and weaknesses. Through intensive prayer, we can easily identify our powerlessness and worthlessness of self. "For I know that in me (that is, in my flesh) dwelleth no good thing: for to will is present with me; but how to perform that which is good I find not" (Rom. 7:18).

7. *Prayer leads to God's inexhaustible store house of divine grace.*

It causes doors that have been closed, to be opened, and open doors of the enemy to be closed. That is the power we find in some of our Pentecostal churches in Africa and other third world countries today, and also in some churches in the western world.

8. *A powerful praying church invokes the presence of God's power in the church or in prayer cells.*

"And call upon me in the day of trouble: I will deliver thee, and thou shalt glorify me" (Psalms 50:15).

"But they that wait upon the Lord shall renew their strength; they shall mount up with wings as eagles; they shall run, and not be weary; and they shall walk, and not faint" (Isaiah 40:31).

We should learn to *"Pray without ceasing"* (1 Thess. 5:17). Our minds and heart should always be focused on the things of God. Our conversations and all that we do, should glorify God.

THE MARKS OF A PRAYING CHURCH

The main problem in our churches today is that we have totally ignored prayers, which should be the inner life of the church. It is prayer that can solve most of our numerous problems, such as choosing the right leaders, fulfilling our financial obligations, getting people from outside to attend our services, securing spiritual results from our ministry, and even the love of God among the children of God. Despite these challenges, the greatest problem of our church today is prayer. If the church can give itself to prayer, many of the other problems will eventually be resolved. Prayer is the life of any church that wants to thrive today. All activities in the church should be centered on prayer. Whether it is worship, paying tithes and offerings, church meetings, or settling disputes, they should be centered on prayer. In Acts 4:23-35, the marks of a praying church were all too apparent. At this time, the gospel was spreading like bush fire, and nobody could stop the message of Jesus Christ. The chief priest and the Pharisees threatened the apostles not to preach or teach in the name of Jesus (Acts 4:18). The secret of the whole story is that they had lived with Jesus. They knew him personally, and they have seen all the miracles and promises of the future. I would like us to observe closely the inner life they enjoyed, and let us ask ourselves: Is my church a praying church?

1. *In a praying church, there is the supreme recognition of prayer, and therefore, there is a spontaneous desire to pray.*

Peter and John were put in jail for preaching the message of our Lord Jesus Christ. When they were released, they went to the company of their fellow Christians, and reported to them what they had gone through (verse 23). When the Christians heard their story, what did they do? They all turned and did what was right in the eyes of the Lord (verse 24). "And when they heard that, they lifted up their voice to God with one accord, and said, Lord, thou art God, which hast made heaven, and earth, and the sea, and all that in them is"

They prayed to the Lord, they recognized the fact that prayer was the most important thing in the life of the ministry. As Christians, do we recognize the supreme importance of prayer? Yes, the church in the book of Acts recognized it. We should also recognize the importance of prayers in our churches today.

2. *In a praying church, faith looks towards the Lord.*

In verse 24, we observe that they did not focus on what Peter and John went through, but they instead focused on the Lord Jesus Christ, whom they all believed will solve all of their problems. In Psalms 62:5, we read, "My soul, wait thou only upon God; for my expectation is from him." Whatever challenges come our way, we should be focused on the Lord for a solution. It is not church meetings, money, and the preacher that matters. These are all secondary. The eyes of a praying church are upon God, who is the sovereign Lord (verse 24), the self-revealing Lord (verse 25), and the seeing Lord (verse 29).

3. *In a praying church, there is obedience to the great commission.*

See how they prayed: "And now, Lord, behold their threatenings: and grant unto thy servants, that with all boldness they may speak thy word" (Acts 4:29). Notice that they did not pray for revenge. They were petitioning that Peter and John should be protected. They were interested in proclaiming the gospel of Jesus Christ, and not on what Peter and John went through. The overwhelming desire of a praying church is to make sure that the gospel is known and heard in the entire world (Matt. 28:19). Does this mark characterize our churches today? Are we making constant efforts to evangelize and get souls to be born again?

4. *In a praying church, there is faith to demand miracles.*

When prayer is top on the agenda in a church, the tendency is that God will break in with supernatural acts. His signs and wonders will follow that church (verse 30). The Christians prayed that God should perform miracles. Apostolic signs and miracles are for the church of Jesus Christ today. There is no iota of truth that miracles are not for the church today. The writer of Hebrews says; "Jesus Christ the same yesterday, and to day, and for ever" (Heb. 13:8). When miracles are wrought in the spiritual realm, souls become saved, and even hardened unbelievers become converted. The sick are healed and saved, and the dead are raised to life.

5. *In a praying church, the Holy Ghost manifests His presence and power.*

Prayer is the secret of any Pentecostal outpouring; but notice, we are not considering what happened at Pentecost. This happened after Pentecost, and it will continue to happen again and again and again!

6. *In a praying church, there is mighty power in Gospel preaching.*

What happened when they had prayed (Acts 4:31 and 33)? This happens in a praying church. People are stricken down by the power of the Word, and multitudes are saved; but in every case where great things have been accomplished through the preaching of the gospel, it has always been in answer to the prayers of God's people. Conviction and conversion follow the preaching, which is backed by a praying church.

7. *In a praying church, there is great grace in the lives of God's people.*

In verse 33, the operative words are "great grace". This grace means "Christlikeness"- and it is seen in four ways:

a. There was the grace of unity (verse 32).
b. There was the grace of renunciation (verse 32).
c. There was the grace of fellowship (verse 32).
d. There was the grace of liberality (verse 34-35).

These are the seven marks of a praying church enumerated above. A praying church, therefore, is a company of Christians who pray, not only individually, but corporately. As Christians, we should make our church a praying church, in order for God to fulfill His purpose in our calling here on earth.

WHY OUR PRAYERS ARE HINDERED

Since the period when God called Israel and made a covenant with them, they have always been grieving the Spirit of the Lord, and rebelling against His authority. The covenant at Sanai has been violated several times by the nation of Israel, and they have been copying the tradition of their neighbors, and marrying their children, whom God had directed them to destroy. A classic example is in the book of Judges. Any time they rebelled against God, they were chastised; and any time they repented and returned to God, they were forgiven and blessed.

King Saul lost his kingdom because of sin. King David almost lost his kingdom to his son, Absalom, because of sin. The scattering of the nation of Israel into Assyria and Babylon was because of sin. Sin hinders our relationship with God. Sin may lead to consequences that none of us could imagine. Being passive also with the things of God, or even being in a church, and still being a skeptic about the miracles that God is performing, is a sin.

In the account of Matthew in the New Testament, we find out that there are certain sins that cannot be forgiven, especially when we sin against the Holy Ghost. The nation of Israel did not believe that Jesus was the Messiah. The worst sin was when they grieved the Holy Spirit, as we find in Matthew 12:22-32. Jesus healed a man that was blind and dumb. Instead of the people and the Jewish leaders appreciating the miracle that Jesus did, they thought He was casting out the demon through the spirit of Beelzebub (the lord of filth), the prince of devils. Jesus could discern their thoughts, and He said to them,

"Every kingdom divided against itself is brought to desolation; and every city or house divided against itself shall not stand: And if Satan cast out Satan, he is divided against himself; how shall then his kingdom stand? And if I by Beelzebub cast out devils, by whom do your children cast them out? Therefore they shall be your judges. But if I cast out devils by the Spirit of God, then the kingdom of God is come unto you. Or else how can one enter into a strong man's house, and spoil his goods, except he first bind the strong man? And then he will spoil his house. He that is not with me is against me; and he that gathereth not with me scattereth abroad. Wherefore I say unto you, All manner of sin and blasphemy shall be forgiven unto men: but the blasphemy against the Holy Ghost shall not be forgiven unto men. And whosoever speaketh a word against the Son of man, it shall be forgiven him: but whosoever speaketh against the Holy Ghost, it shall not be forgiven him, neither in this world, neither in the world to come"

This is Matthews account. Let us now look at Mark's account.

"And when his friends heard of it, they went out to lay hold on him: for they said, he is beside himself. And the Scribes which came down from Jerusalem said, he hath Beelzebub, and by the prince of the devils casteth he out devils" (Mark 3:21-22). In other words, they were saying that Jesus has an unclean spirit. What a blasphemy against the Holy Ghost! There are churches today who do not believe in miracles. Such a disbelief hinders the power of God in the church. When they see what is happening in other Pentecostal churches, they still accuse the people of pretending in order to lure people in their church. Prayers can be hindered in the church because of several reasons.

1. *There may be serious disagreements among the Christians and the church leaders; it may be due to doctrines that are biblically unfounded, or due to envy among the Christians, etc.*

2. *Sometimes, God hears our prayers, but the devil does everything to hinder what God has planned for us.*

Satan can stand in the way of an answered prayer, as we find in the book of Daniel 10:11-13. Daniel was fasting and praying for three full weeks when the angel of the Lord appeared to him; "And he said unto me, O Daniel; a man greatly beloved, understand the words I speak unto thee, and stand upright: for unto thee am I now sent. And when he had spoken this word unto me, I stood trembling. Then he said unto me, Fear not, Daniel: for from the first day that thou didst set thine heart to understand, and to chasten thyself before thy God, thy words were heard, and I am come for thy words. But the prince of the kingdom of Persia withstood me one and twenty days: but, lo, Michael, one of the chief princes, came to help me; and I remained there with the kings of Persia" (Dan.

10:11-13). The answer to a hindered prayer is found in Ephesians 6:10-18. The formula to combat Satan is found in Isaiah 40:31. "But they that wait upon the Lord shall renew their strength; they shall mount up with wings as eagles; they shall run, and not be weary; and they shall walk, and not faint."

3. *Prayers may also be hindered when Christians indulge themselves in worldly activities, such as partying with unbelievers, lotteries in the church, bazaars, and memorial services.*

Those were things of the world that have now found themselves in our churches, and they are organized by the church. There are also Christians attending gambling events with unbelievers. Boy Scouts and Girl Guides in the church do grieve the Spirit of God. As Christians, we are to resist such activities.

The argument some Christians give is that if we rely entirely on the teachings of the Bible, and practicing them without indulging in some of these activities, then they may end up driving many people out of the church. This type of attitude is what Stephen pointed out to the Jews before he was stoned to death: "Ye stiffnecked and uncircumcised in heart and ears, ye do always resist the Holy Ghost: as your fathers did, so do ye." (Acts 7:51). Many people, instead of yielding or being led by the Holy Spirit, they are instead grieving the Holy Spirit. The apostle Paul warned the church in Ephesus against this attitude.

(Eph. 4:30-31).

The church today has derailed from its calling, and is guilty of grieving the Holy Spirit. Revival has been dampened, and they do not know what to do. The problem today is that many people do not know what it means to be called. The large crowd we sometimes find in the church does not bring glory to God. They are still a menace to the plan of God. What are we to do? We are to go back to the apostolic teachings, and those who want to leave, can very well do so, and they should do it very quickly. A remnant that is called can take over the world by storm through prayers. Prayer is a difficult task, but it is the only way forward for the spiritual growth of the church.

4. *The choir in the church can either be a blessing or a curse to the church.*

My personal experience is that some people creep to positions to lead the choir, and we do not pray to God to find out whether they are the right people. An anointed choir can sing, and some people will be shedding tears because they have been moved by the Holy Spirit, while a dead choir can sing, and people will instead be sleeping or are distracted by one thing or the other. It is important that we always pray and allow the Holy Spirit to do its work rather than us humans. The choir should always pray seriously for the Lord to do its miracle in their midst and also in the church.

5. *The prayer team can be a hindrance to the church.*

Its leaders should be people of prayer. Members of the prayer team should be members full of the Holy Ghost, and are well known and respected by members of the church. When people of dubious character or members from the occult world or witches find themselves in the prayer team, that church will be in big trouble. No matter what prayers you pray, those contrary spirits will hold your prayers down.

6. *Our prayers are sometimes hindered when we pray with wrong motives.*

When we are praying for a selfish reason, God will not answer such prayers. "Ye ask, and receive not, because ye ask amiss, that ye may consume it upon your lusts" (James 4:3).

WHAT SHOULD ACCOMPANY PRAYERS

Prayers should always be accompanied by:

a. Watching or being alert (Luke 21:36; 1 Pet. 4:7; Col. 4, 2).
b. Confessions of personal and corporate sins (James 5:16).
c. Repentance (1 Kings 8:33; Jer. 36:7)
d. Fasting (Neh. 1:4; Dan. 9:3; Acts 13:3).
e. Praise (Psalms 66:17).
f. Thanks giving (Phil. 4:6; Col. 4:2)
g. Proclamation (Psalms 48:13; 18:3, 46; 116:1-2).

SPIRITUAL DISCERNMENT

One of the greatest challenges Christians face is how to discern the Spirit of God or the will of God in whatever they do in their daily lives. The level of discernment in our life depends greatly on our yielding to the Spirit of God.

In the first chapter, we discussed the differences between the spirit, soul, and body, and how they interplay with each other. In this chapter, we will first deal with how the state of your spirit will determine how much we can discern the mind of God, and then later we will deal with how Christians can learn how to discern situations, which is in consonance with the mind of God. The greatest challenge men and women of God face is that they must allow the Spirit of God to take preeminence in all their decision making. It is when we are determined to allow the Spirit of God to rule over our flesh, that our discernment becomes very clear. The error that most people make is that they think that what comes to their mind is really what God is leading them to do. When your mind or your emotions determine your life, then it is the flesh that is in control of your life. This therefore means that you are unfit to do God's work. We must learn to break away from the flesh, and then allow the spirit of God to be released in us. When the flesh is in control of your spirit, your receptivity becomes very weak, because it is the flesh that is in control of the spirit. Many people think that if we are children of God, things automatically change, and you are in the perfect will of God. Some believe that if you have been with the Lord for a long time or you are a church leader, your discernment is that of the Lord. This is absolutely false! It is the purity of your spirit that will determine whether what you discern is from the Lord. No matter how spiritually powerful you are; or no matter how much you fast and pray; or no matter how much God uses you, if you do not submit to the spirit, you have missed the mark of your calling. I know that we are living in a democratic society, but it is not the majority that is always right. You may be in the minority, and God will be revealing deep things to you, which are contrary to what the leaders of the church believe. The state of your spirit will determine whether you will discern the right thing. The apostle Paul said in Romans chapter 7:22; "For I delight in the law of God after the inward man."

The apostle Paul caught the truth of how he can receive from the spirit, and his spirit will then be in tune with that of the Lord. That is why he went further to say in 2 Corinthians 4:16; "But though our outer man perish, yet the inward man is renewed day by day. "We renew our inward man which is the spirit of God in us, by leaning to the Word of God, and applying it in our lives every day in whatever decisions we make. The Bible makes a clear distinction between the flesh and the Spirit. When we lean towards the Spirit of God, our receptivity in the Spirit becomes very high and very acute. That is why the apostle Paul said in Galatians 5:17; "For the flesh lusteth against the Spirit, and the Spirit against the flesh: and these are contrary the one to the other: so that ye cannot do the things that ye would."

The Spirit and the flesh are always in a constant battle. It is when we submit to the Spirit of God in our lives, that our Spiritual receptivity becomes very high, and we can discern the will of God in our lives. Let me take for example that a sister or a brother wants to get married. They go to the pastor or to any of the church leaders in the church, and present their problem to them. The Lord may have been directing them to marry somebody who may not be a very serious brother or sister as the church may think, but that is what they have been discerning or receiving from the Lord. They take it to the pastor or whoever is the leader of the church, and he now advises him to marry someone who is more serious in the Lord. After marriage for a couple of years, the divine will now becomes God's permissive will. Who will we blame? The pastor, God, or yourself? The will of God in your life has been deadened by a wrong decision. How do you know that the sister or brother you have been given by the Lord for marriage, will become a spiritual giant tomorrow? I am not talking about marrying an unbeliever. An unbeliever will always convert you, the believer. I will never advise a Christian to marry an unbeliever.

For a Christian to have a high spirit of discernment, the Spirit must suppress the flesh. Lest we forget, there is a clear divide between the Spirit and the flesh. If we are true children of God, we must allow the flesh to be in total subjection to the Spirit.

HOW TO DISCERN

In the world we live, we know people, and the way they live and do things. We can easily discern what decision they will take when something happens to them. The Lord Jesus Christ could discern who Judas Iscariot was. He knew that he was a thief, and that he will betray Him at the end of His ministry here on earth. It is the same thing with our spouses. We know how they will react in certain situations. They have been living with us for some time, and we could judge their temperament when situations arise. The problem we will face is, how will you judge people whom you meet for the first time? In the case of the damsel whom Paul met for the first time, the apostle could discern that the spirit she possessed was not the Holy Spirit (Acts 16). The damsel was telling the truth about Paul and others, but the apostle could discern that there was something not right with her. Paul wasted no time in rebuking the spirit, which left her the same hour.

Before we became Christians, we could discern situations because of the experiences we have encountered in life. When we became believers in Christ, we depend on the leading of the Holy Spirit, to know situations or people. If we encounter people for the first time, just as Paul met the damsel, something will burn inside you that gives you no rest. Paul knew that there was something not right. Have you found yourself in such a situation? Yes, I know you have; however, in certain people, the Spirit has not yet taken over the flesh. The cloak of the flesh is still suppressing the Spirit of God in them because they are still full of self.

God wants us to discern situations, and know how to handle them. Our fleshly desires will always want to suppress our spirit. The flesh needs to be broken, if we are to have a high level of discernment. You cannot say that you are a child of God, and you want to satisfy your own desires, and think that God will accept it. The outward man needs to be broken, to allow the inward man to reign in your life.

There is something that believers need to know, and that is that the spirit in you must assume a new function. The Spirit of God is very sensitive because it bears God's nature. The Spirit of God is meant for us to use in our everyday life. It is important that we break the flesh, and allow the spirit to commune easily with the Spirit of God. God wants you to function in this new role, where you exercise your spirit in everything you do. When you allow your spirit to discern, the flesh must be quiet. Do not allow preconceived ideas to reign in you. When the spirit in you is in control of the flesh, any wrong ideas coming into you will be rebuffed by the spirit. The sad situation is that many of us have developed our own righteousness, which has impaired the righteousness of God in us. If our spirit is quiet in a tumultuous situation, it will be easier for us to discern the right thing. It is the spirit in you that must discern, and not the flesh.

There comes a challenge; suppose you find yourself in a large congregation, and they are deciding over a situation that your spirit completely rejects? Will you follow the crowd, and be quiet over it, or will you present your own inner man to them? As children of God, we need to hold tenaciously to our spirit, rather than being influenced by others, when it comes to things of the spirit. The apostle Paul had this to say; "Therefore, my beloved brethren, be ye steadfast, unmovable, always abounding in the work of the Lord, forasmuch as ye know that your labour is not in vain in the Lord" (1 Cor. 15:58). As children of God, we are not to give in to others, for what we know is right in the eyes of God. If you are in a church where people are divided over a situation, what position will you take? Do you just want to be in the majority or minority, or will you take the position of your spirit? As a child of God, you are not to waiver or please anybody. I will want us to look at two personalities: Paul and Peter. Peter was a man who will waiver sometimes to please the crowd. Paul was not. He never gave in to anything that he knew was wrong. In Galatians 2:14-16, we find Peter compromising with the Jews in order to please them, but Paul was the opposite. He blasted Peter before all. He did not spare his double standards. There is something to learn here. Paul wanted to make it clear that Christianity is no longer under the law. We are now living under grace. Paul was defending the special revelation that he had from the Lord, when he withdrew to Arabia to understand this new religion, at the time he was struck down by the Lord on his way to Damascus (Gal. 1:17). As Christians, when we get a special revelation from the Lord, it is your duty to defend it. Don't be carried away by the majority. The majority is not always right. Our calling must be defended at all cost. Your foundation is in Christ, and not in man. Why do people like Peter always stumble? It may be that they want to please the crowd; or they are afraid of criticism from others; or because of the fear of rejection. As children of God, once you know the truth, you have to defend it at all cost.

Spiritual discernment is not an easy task. Sometimes, we may confuse our spiritual discipline and spiritual discernment. We may grow up to be disciplined in the things of God, but discerning things in some situations is quite different. Spiritual discipline may lead you to a better quality of life. As Christians, we have to develop an accurate spirit. Knowing the truth can only come through God's revelation in your life. It does not come from how long you have been with the Lord, or your level of education, or your experiences in life. Direct revelation from God comes with a quiet voice that will strike you from within. It comes like a fire in your inner man. It comes with great conviction. It has nothing to do with your thoughts. Great revelations sometimes may occur only once or twice in your lifetime.

As children of God, we should not allow our emotions to control us. If this happens to you, then it is the soul that is reigning over you. As children of God, the spirit must always be preeminent. We must always allow our spirit man to dictate our emotions. Have you been in a situation where something happens, and you are very angry, but at the same time, you hear a quiet voice talking to you? God will speak with a quiet voice, or sometimes you see certain Scripture verses coming to your mind spontaneously. That is God wanting to take control over your emotions (soul). The reaction of an individual in certain situations will let you know whether the person is of the right spirit or not. A rash reaction is not of God.

DISCOVERING THE TRUTH

One of the greatest things any believer should do is abide by the truth. It is by abiding by the Word of God that you will be able to know the truth. The apostle John had this to say, "If any man will do his will, he shall know of the doctrine, whether it be of God, or whether I speak of myself" (John 7:17). When we read further in the book of John, Jesus Himself said to those Jews that have believed him, "If ye continue in my word, then are ye my disciples indeed; and ye shall know the truth, and the truth shall make you free" (John 8:31-32). Since the Word of God is the truth, then everything in it is truth. Amen. We are bound to the Word because it is absolute. If we say we are bound to it, then we are to do what is written in it. This is what will mold your character to the extent that people will see that you are a changed person; you are now a spiritual being. However, we have to be careful as we discover the truth. We are not to be selective. We may even have to hold on to the things that we may not necessarily like. We are not to choose what we like from what we do not like. We are bound to the Word because we are all bondmen and bondwomen. A slave does not go against his master's will...Everything is yea and not nay.

As we discover the truth, we should know that our experience counts. Our lives ten years ago cannot be the same as today. You have become matured to the things of God. You can understand your environment more now than you could ten years ago.

If we know the truth, we have to say it in black and white. Do not sugar-coat it; if you do that, you will be leaving your brother or sister in darkness. In the Old Testament, Aaron's two sons, Nadab and Abihu, offered a strange fire, and they died. What did Aaron do? He maintained his peace in order to allow the glory of God to be in place. Moses had to advise the other two sons, Eleazar and

Ithamar, to keep away their feelings, and to maintain God's truth (Lev. 10:1-7). There is a lesson for us to learn here,

1. Do not allow your own personality (soul) to take control of the Spirit of God, which is the absolute truth.
2. Learn to distinguish between love and hate, which may interfere with the Word of God.
3. Do not focus so much on material things. They may be important, but they should not control you.
4. Humility in Christ should be your goal. Do not allow yourself to be exalted before men.

8

SPEAKING IN TONGUES

Speaking in tongues is a God-given sign, which is followed by the manifestation of the Holy Spirit. It is rather unfortunate that many churches of our day have rejected this gift for reasons which are biblically flawed. Tongues are a Spirit-inspired utterance, whereby believers in Christ speak a God-given language. Tongues are not a language you learn; they are a Spirit-inspired utterance. They are not an "ecstatic utterance", as some Christians claim them to be. The reason for the gift of tongues, is that God wants to have a close communion with His children. It is one of the means in which God wants to communicate with His people, as we see in Isaiah 28:11: "For with stammering lips and another tongue will he speak to these people."

Yes! Tongues are unknown languages to man, or a heavenly language used by God to talk to humans. It is one of the greatest blessings that God has given to His children. God is all powerful, and His wisdom concerning tongues is unquestionable. It is a gift that Satan has used to deceive many today, to believe that it is no longer useful. However, we have to understand that God's wisdom is wiser than man. What God does in our lives has a clear objective, and that objective is to make us "partakers of His divine nature"

(2 Pet, 1:4). God wants His children to be a reflection of His Son Jesus Christ. He wants us to partake in His glory, as it is written in 2 Corinthians 3:18: "But we all, with open face beholding as in a glass the glory of the Lord, are changed into the same image from glory to glory, even as by the Spirit of the Lord."

TONGUES AND THE BAPTISM OF THE HOLY SPIRIT

It took me two years after I had believed, that I received the baptism of the Holy Spirit, and started speaking in tongues. The experience I had was that I always saw myself speaking in tongues in my dreams, and also fighting great battles in the spirit, but in the physical, I was not speaking in tongues. One day, I was kneeling on the bed, and wanted to commit the night to the Lord before going to bed. Suddenly, I felt some power coming from above like fire, and burning throughout my entire body. I started speaking in tongues, and shivering as tears were running down my eyes.

After my experience, I asked the Lord why it took so long for me to receive the baptism of the Holy Spirit. The Lord told me that the devil was fighting against it because he knew the havoc that will take place in the kingdom of darkness. This experience was a fulfillment of Acts 2:4. "And they were all filled with the Holy Ghost, and began to speak with other tongues, as the Spirit gave them utterance."

From that day, any time I want to pray, tongues will suddenly come into my spirit, and I will start praying violently in that heavenly language. As time went on, I was praying more in tongues than before, as "rivers of water" poured out of me. "He that believeth on me, as the scripture hath said, out of his belly shall flow rivers of living water. (But this spake he of the Spirit, which they that believe on him should receive: for the Holy Ghost was not yet given; because that Jesus was not yet glorified)" (John 7:38-39).

BENEFITS OF PRAYING IN TONGUES

If God decides to baptize His children in tongues, what are we going to benefit out of it? There should be a reason or several reasons why God will want His children to benefit from speaking in tongues.

1. *It helps us to understand the role of diversities of tongues in God's government.*

"He that descended is the same also that ascended up far above all heavens, that he might fill all things. And he gave some, apostles; and some, prophets; and some, evangelists; and some, pastors and teachers; For the perfecting of the saints, for the work of the ministry, for the edifying of the body of Christ: Till we all come in the unity of the faith, and of the knowledge of the Son of God, unto a perfect man, unto the measure of the statue of the fullness of Christ" (Eph. 4:10-13). God has given fivefold ministries for the edification of the body of Christ. That is the power that Jesus gave to the church, so that it could be properly governed, and also for the perfecting of the saints. The work of the church is not only for some trained officials in the church; it is entirely for the body of Christ. Everybody has a role to play in the ministry. They are supposed to be trained and released, so that multiplication, edification, and growth of the church, should be accomplished as the New Testament pattern.

2. *The church is also to grow into spiritual maturity, and be filled with all the fullness of Christ.*

They are not supposed to be children, tossed to and fro, with the doctrine of men. They are instead to have the knowledge of the truth, by which they will reject any false doctrine or false teachers in their midst.

The tragedy with our churches today is that we think that it is only the pastor and other leaders of the church, that are called. They are treated with such respect, that they do not know that every Christian in the house of God has a calling, and we are all to contribute for the spiritual growth of the church. The medical doctors, lawyers, pharmacists, nurses, teachers, professors, farmers, market traders who sell all sorts of items to survive, engineers, and other people in all walks of life, also have the call of God in their lives. The fact that one has gone to a seminary and Bible college, does not make him or her spiritually superior to other Christians. We are all co-equals in Christ, and God has given special gifts to all his children, who have turned to Him in obedience. God has brought us together to be united, but man has brought division in the church. There are several gifts for the church, and God has blessed His children with these gifts, to lay a solid foundation for the church (1 Cor. 12:24-31).

THE FOUR BASIC DIVERSITIES OF TONGUES

One of the greatest blessings that I received as a Christian, was that I was well grounded in the bible by the Scripture Union in the University of Port Harcourt. I knew the importance of speaking in tongues. As a new Christian, I was praying for it to manifest in my life, so that I can use it as often as possible.

I knew that through the use of tongues, I will effectively operate in the Spirit, and receive greater revelations. This finally manifested itself when it came. I realized that I could seek the face of the Lord, as I was on my knees for a very long time, without knowing. The burden of praying in the Spirit became more frequent, and the Lord was revealing deep things about my life and my future.

The different diversities of tongues are as follows:

1. *Tongues for personal edification (1 Cor. 14:2).*

"For he that speaketh in an unknown tongue speaketh not unto men, but unto God: for no man understandeth him; howbeit in the spirit he speaketh mysteries." In the previous chapter, the apostle Paul advised the Corinthians to prefer charity over all spiritual gifts. In chapter 14, he changes the conversation, and directs them on which spiritual gifts they should covet; and that is speaking in tongues for personal edification. This is a heavenly language when we are filled with the Holy Ghost.

Tongues for personal edification is a means by which the believer communicates directly to God in private or in the church, through prayer, praise, worship, blessings, and thanks giving. Tongues for personal edification does great things in our lives, that it is only you alone who can testify what God has done in your life. We can receive all the great teachings from the Bible teacher or pastor, but that experience is only you and you alone. You can use tongues at your own discretion. My personal experience with speaking in tongues, is that the more I use it, the more God will reveal deeper things in the spirit, which in my own natural self, I would not believe that such things are true. I remember a sister who wanted to know who really were her close friends, and those who were her enemies. She prayed in tongues for a very long time, and slept. That night, she could not believe what she saw. One of her closest friends, whom she was even exchanging clothes with, was attempting to kill her. The Lord revealed to her all of her plans, and she was told by the Lord to withdraw from that relationship.

There was another brother who was walking through a bush path. The Holy Spirit told him to pray in tongues. He obeyed, and started praying; he continued for about thirty minutes, and the spirit told him to stop. The following day, a man approached him, and asked who was he calling at that particular moment, and how did he know that he was hiding in the bush? In fact, the man was planning to attack him, but was frightened, and escaped because he thought the man knew he was hiding in the bush, and was planning to attack him. What a miracle!

2. *Tongues for interpretation (1 Cor. 14:5).*

I would that ye all spake with tongues, but rather that ye prophesied: for greater is he that prophesieth than he that speaketh with tongues, except he interpret, that the church may receive edifying." In many situations, we have heard of people speaking in tongues, and another person is interpreting it in the church or in a prayer cell. This is a particular gift that God has blessed some people with. We can all speak in an unknown tongue, but not everybody in the body of Christ can interpret it. Interpretation of tongues mostly takes place when the body of Christ is praying in a tongue, and somebody starts interpreting it. This had occurred to me when I was praying in the spirit, and suddenly a pastor, who is a friend of mine, started interpreting what I was praying.

3. *Tongues of deep intercessional groanings (Rom. 8:26).*

"Likewise the Spirit also helpeth our infirmities: for we know not what we should pray for as we ought: but the Spirit itself maketh intercession for us with groanings which cannot be uttered." Intercessory prayer is a holy, believing, preserving prayer, whereby someone stands on the gap to intervene for somebody or some people. In Daniel 9, Daniel was interceding for the restoration of the nation of Israel. In both the Old and New Testaments, there are many occurrences whereby people have stood on the gap to pray to God, so that He can intervene in a situation, where man can do nothing but only wait for a miracle to take place. In the Old Testament, we have notable leaders, such as kings, prophets, and priests, who led prayers for the nation. Abraham interceded for Sodom and Gomorrah (Gen. 18:23-32); David's prayer for a son (2 Sam. 12:16; 1 Chron. 29:19); Ezra's prayer (Ezra 9:5-15), etc.

In the New Testament, Christ prayed for those He came to seek and to save (Luke 19:10). Jesus wept over the city of Jerusalem (Luke 19:41).

The present aspect of Christ's ministry is to intervene on our behalf before God's throne (Rom. 8:34; Heb. 7:27: 9:24). The apostle John calls Jesus our *"advocate with the father"* (1 John 2:1).

The epistles of Paul are full of intercessory prayers. Paul prayed for the different churches and individuals (Rom. 1:9-10; 2 1cor. 13:7; Phil. 1:4-7; Col. 1:3, 9-12 etc.).

There are also moments when we are called by God to intervene for others, or even for ourselves. Sometimes God will wake me up in the night, and will tell me to pray. God will not tell me the specific reasons why he wants me to pray. In such instances, I will pray in tongues, as the spirit leads me.

There are moments in which I have prayed for people who were sick. My experience is that when I meet people with terminal diseases, I pray in tongues for at least an hour, while laying my hands on them. In some cases, I have prayed through people's pictures, and they received their healing. If I do not have their picture, I write down their full names, and lay my hands on them, and pray in tongues for a very long time. I have received a lot of testimonies through these means of interceding for others.

4. *Tongues are a sign to the unbeliever (1 Cor. 14:22).*

"Wherefore tongues are for a sign, not to them that believe, but to them that believe not: but prophesying serveth not for them that believe not, but for them which believe." Tongues become a sign to the unbeliever because he realizes that he is out of place. Tongues make the unbeliever to think that he is separated from Christ, and cannot understand what is taking place.

Prophecy, however, is a sign to the believer because they recognize the supernatural work of the Holy Spirit, and that God is at work in the church today, as it was at the time of the apostles.

Unbelievers sometimes have believed in the Lord, when someone prayed in tongues, and another person prophesied the problem that the unbeliever was facing, and how his problem can be resolved.

DO ALL SPEAK IN TONGUES?

"Are all apostles? Are all prophets? Are all teachers? Are all workers of miracles? Have all the gifts of healing? Do all speak with tongues? Do all interpret? But covet earnestly the best gifts: and yet shew I unto you a more excellent way" (1 Cor. 12:29-31). The apostle Paul is asking a rhetorical question here, and the answer is that all of us cannot have all the gifts. Not every Christian can have the gift of miracles, but we are called to fulfill Mark 16:17-18.

"And these signs shall follow them that believe; in my name shall they cast out devils; they shall speak with new tongues; They shall take up serpents; and if they drink any deadly thing, it shall not hurt them; they shall lay hands on the sick, and they shall recover." It is rather unfortunate that there are some people who do not believe in speaking in tongues, because they say that Paul asked the question; *"Do all speak in tongues?"* They say that this gift is not for everybody, and as a result, they feel that they do not need it. If this is true, then let's look at Acts 2:4; the apostles and the new converts were filled by the Holy Spirit, and spoke in tongues. In Acts 10:44-46, Cornelius and his household were filled with the Holy Spirit, and spoke in tongues. In Acts 19:2-6, all who were filled with the Holy Spirit, spoke in tongues.

Every believer is supposed to speak in tongues, but not every believer has the nine gifts of the Holy Spirit.

Printed in the United States
By Bookmasters